Wilson On Wine 2015

THE WINES TO DRINK THIS YEAR

IRISH TIMES BOOKS

in association with

Santa Rita

Published by: The Irish Times Limited
Editor: Joe Breen
Design & Layout: Angelo McGrath.
Photographer: Marc O'Sullivan

ISBN: 978 0 9070 11439

Wilson On Wine 2015

THE WINES TO DRINK THIS YEAR

I taste a huge number of wines every year. You find the odd shocker that should never have been allowed past the cellar door. But the vast majority are fine – nothing more and nothing less. Then you come across the really good stuff, wines that excite and set your pulse racing with their amazing range of flavours and wonderful complexity. This book is about those wines.

This is a personal selection from the thousands I tasted over the last year or so. Why 123? Well, selecting wine for a guide sounds as easy as 123 but, in reality, there were lots of tough choices - I uncovered many great bottles in 2014!

The wines had to be available and, in most cases, reasonably priced. There aren't many under €12, but, with our taxes, the more interesting wines are always going to cost more than this. Of the 123 wines, well over half cost €20 or less, giving everyone plenty of options at an affordable price.

I have tried to ensure the prices quoted are accurate. However, this book goes to print before Budget 2014; if the Minister for Finance increases excise duty once more, or if producers increase their prices in early 2015, there may be discrepancies.

You will notice that there are very few wines from the supermarkets. This is partly down to the way they buy and sell wine; their range tends to be seasonal, or features once-off parcels of wine. These can be great value, but won't always be available. The prices change with lightening speed too. Put all of these factors together and it was hard to find wines with real character that would be available at the same price for the next six months.

That doesn't mean I don't enjoy their wines. Nor does it mean the multiples cannot offer eclectic wines; some of them are very good at this. I am not, I hope, a wine snob, but I do believe that the more interesting wines tend to be made by smaller producers and these are most often found in independent wine shops and off-licences. Wherever you shop, you should be able to get your hands on these wines without too much trouble.

I am grateful to Santa Rita and The Irish Times for sponsoring this book; simply put, without their support it wouldn't have happened.

So here you have it – my favourite 123 wines for 2015. I hope you find the book fun to read and discover new and exciting wines along the way.

Happy drinking!

John Wilson

Jwilson@irishtimes.com
www.wilsononwine.ie

IRISH TIMES BOOKS

in association with

Santa Rita

THE WINE STYLES

Describing wines is never easy or exact; one person's cherries can be another's plums. I have tried to keep the tasting notes as short as possible and to avoid very florid descriptions. I hope that they will give you a real sense of the wine's taste. I also give a possible food match with each wine, some fairly specific but most are very broad suggestions. Matching food and wine can be complicated. It is not just about the main constituent of a meal; the sauce, the accompanying vegetables, fruits and herbs all make a difference. I do include quite a few all-purpose wines that can be happily matched with most foods.Instead of simply listing the wines in price order or by country, I think it more useful to divide them up by style; this should make it easier to access the kind of wine you like, and to encourage you to experiment a little. The categories are also colour-coded to aid navigation.

SPARKLING WINES 1-22
Self-explanatory I hope!

CRISP REFRESHING WHITE WINES 23-64
Light, zesty dry white wines with plenty of refreshing acidity. They generally have less alcohol and lighter fruits than those in the Fresh & Fruity category. Good to drink on their own, or with lighter dishes.

FRESH AND FRUITY WHITE WINES 65-102
White wines with plenty of mouth-watering fruits balanced by good acidity. Generally unoaked, with more fruit and flavour than the Crisp Refreshing Whites. Fine to drink on their own or with richer fish and salad dishes.

RICH AND ROUNDED WHITE WINES 103-122
Bigger, more powerful textured white wines, some oak-aged, that fill the mouth with flavour. These wines are best served alongside food.

LIGHT AND ELEGANT RED WINES 123-170
Restrained, lighter wines with more subtle fruits. They are lower in alcohol and have light tannins. These can be drunk on their own or with lighter foods.

ROUNDED AND FRUITY RED WINES 171-220
These red wines have plenty of smooth rounded fruits and moderate tannins; good with many foods.

RICH AND FULL-BODIED RED WINES 221-248
The biggest and most powerful red wines, robust and rich in alcohol and flavour. Some have high levels of tannin too. These wines are best drunk alongside substantial dishes.

FORTIFIED WINES 249-262
Wines such as sherry, port and madeira receive a fortifying boost of brandy to increase their alcohol in the winemaking process. A great many are dry, others are sweet, but don't ignore them - these are amongst the most complex wines of all, and some go really well with food too.

SPARKLING

1

Aldi Cava Contevedo
Brut NV
Spain 11.5% **€10.49**

STOCKISTS: Aldi

Aldi Cava Contevedo
Brut NV

TASTING NOTE
Zesty and fresh with creamy green fruits, this is one of
the best-value bottles of fizz I have tasted in some time.

DRINK WITH
Friends at a party

STYLE
Sparkling

GRAPE VARIETY
Macabeo, Xarello, Chardonnay

BACKSTORY
I haven't always been a great fan of Cava. Too often this
Spanish sparkling wine smelled of wet cardboard. Either
it has mellowed or I have, but over the last few years I
have come across some very well-made fruit-filled wines
that make a very pleasant change from Prosecco.

2

Jacob's Creek
Sparkling Non Vintage Rosé
Australia 11.5% **€18.49**

STOCKISTS: Widely available including Dunnes,
SuperValu and Tesco.

Jacob's Creek
Sparkling Non Vintage Rosé

TASTING NOTE
Juicy fresh cherries and redcurrants with plenty of frothy
bubbles.

DRINK WITH
Nibbles or at celebratory lunches.

STYLE
Sparkling

GRAPE VARIETY
Chardonnay Pinot Noir

BACKSTORY
Friends rarely give me a gift of wine; they figure (correctly)
that I am not short of a bottle or two. However, I received
a bottle of the JC rosé fizz recently and, on a warm
summery evening, it was just perfect. But then I am a
big fan of the Jacob's Creek sparkling wines; they are
seriously good value for money.

3

Jeio Prosecco Spumante
Valdobiaedenne NV
Italy 11% **€26.60**

STOCKISTS: Searsons, Monkstown; Jus de Vine,
Portmarnock; 1601, Kinsale

Jeio Prosecco Spumante
Valdobiaedenne NV

TASTING NOTE
Fresh pear and peach fruits with a good lively citrus edge.

DRINK WITH
Friends as an aperitif

STYLE
Sparkling

GRAPE VARIETY
Glera

BACKSTORY
Prosecco has been the success story of recession Ireland. Cheaper than most sparkling wines, it offers bubbles at a bargain price. However, step up and the more expensive versions can be very good. More accessible than Champagne, they offer high-quality fruit and a lovely freshness such as this fine example. This one would be wasted in a Bellini; drink it chilled with friends when you have something to celebrate.

4

Beaumont de Crayères
Grande Réserve N.V. Champagne
France 12% **€36.99**

STOCKISTS: O'Briens

Beaumont de Crayères
Grande Réserve N.V. Champagne

TASTING NOTE
A good reliable Champagne with plenty of ripe, rounded redcurrant and apple fruits and a decent finish.

DRINK WITH
Fish, shellfish and nibbles. Also works well as an aperitif.

STYLE
Sparkling

GRAPE VARIETY
Chardonnay, Pinot Noir

BACKSTORY
O'Briens has been offering Beaumont de Crayères for many years, and with good reason. The name may not have the recognition factor of the bigger brands, but the wines really stand up - they are well-made and nicely balanced at prices that are very fair.

5

Oudinot Brut
Champagne NV
France 12% **€39**

STOCKISTS: Marks & Spencer

Oudinot Brut
Champagne NV

TASTING NOTE
An appetising crisp, dry Champagne with cool green fruits and a touch of toasted brioche. For posh celebrations.

DRINK WITH
Shellfish or canapés; possibly a little austere to serve on its own.

STYLE
Sparkling

GRAPE VARIETY
Chardonnay

BACKSTORY
This is a Blanc de Blancs Champagne made entirely from Chardonnay - others will be a blend with Pinot Noir and/or Pinot Meunier. Blanc de Blanc tends to be lighter and fresher but it develops a wonderful seductive biscuity toastiness with a little age.

6

Larmandier Bernier
Latitude Extra Brut
NV, Champagne
France 12% **€59.50**

STOCKISTS: Terroirs, Donnybrook, Dublin

Larmandier Bernier
Latitude Extra Brut NV, Champagne

TASTING NOTE
Succulent ripe fruits cut through with a delicious
minerality and great length.

DRINK WITH
You could drink it solo, but Champagne is a very versatile
food wine – and heavenly with oysters.

STYLE
Sparkling

14

GRAPE VARIETY
Chardonnay, Pinot Noir, Pinot Meunier

BACKSTORY
Pierre and Sophie Larmandier produce small quantities
of the most wonderful precise Champagnes, following
biodynamic practices (very unusual in Champagne). Lower
levels of sugar give these wines an enchanting austere
purity. Check them out.

7

Louis Roederer Brut
Premier NV Champagne
France 12% **€59.99**

15

STOCKISTS: Off-licences nationwide including Ardkeen,
Waterford; The Vintry, Dublin; Mortons, Galway; Karwig,
Cork and O'Briens.

Louis Roederer Brut
Premier NV Champagne

TASTING NOTE
Elegant, yet full of complex toasty fruits and an inviting creamy texture; superb Champagne.

DRINK WITH
A glass before dinner with tasty canapés or smoked salmon.

STYLE
Sparkling

GRAPE VARIETY
Chardonnay, Pinot Noir, Pinot Meunier

BACKSTORY
Champagne company Louis Roederer are best known for its luxury cuvée, Cristal. However, the entire range is faultless starting with the multi-vintage Brut Premier that will cost you less than a third of the price of Cristal. So €60 can be a bargain!

8

Wiston Rosé 2011
South Downs
England 12% **€61.95**

STOCKISTS: Ballymaloe Farm Shop, Cork

Wiston Rosé 2011
South Downs

TASTING NOTE
A delectable strawberry-scented dry wine that I would prefer to many a Champagne.

DRINK WITH
Friends - a great aperitif

STYLE
Sparkling

GRAPE VARIETY
Pinot Noir, Chardonnay

BACKSTORY
English sparkling wine has been making headlines for a number of years. Leaving aside the understandable national pride of some UK journalists (every country suffers from it), there are some seriously good English sparkling wines – at fairly serious prices too. Limerick-born Dermot Sugrue makes a number of excellent sparkling wines for Wiston Estate on the South Downs and for his own label Sugrue Pierre (his wife is a Pierre). For a Wine Geese tasting held in the Ballymaloe pop-up shop in Brown Thomas Cork, Dermot brought over this fine example.

9

Charles Heidseick
Brut Réserve NV Champagne
France 12% **€65**

STOCKISTS: Clontarf Wines; 64wine, Glasthule;
Donnybrook Fair; The Drink Store, Dublin 7; Redmond's,
Ranelagh; Jus de Vine, Portmarnock; La Touche,
Greystones; O'Briens; Sweeney's, Glasnevin; The
Corkscrew, Chatham St.; Thomas, Foxrock; World Wide
Wines, Waterford.

Charles Heidseick
Brut Réserve NV Champagne

TASTING NOTE
A beautifully rich, generous Champagne with nuts and toasted brioche.

DRINK WITH
Friends before dinner or with a plate of prosciutto, almonds and cheesy puffs.

STYLE
Sparkling

GRAPE VARIETY
Chardonnay, Pinot Noir, Pinot Meunier

BACKSTORY
Although Charles Heidseick is not the best-known of the Grande Marque Champagne houses, people in the know will tell you that it is consistently one of the best non-vintage wines, frequently out-performing some of the better-known (and more expensive) brands.

10

Bollinger RD 2002
Champagne
France 12% **€190**

STOCKISTS: Mitchell & Son; 64wine, Glasthule;
The Parting Glass, Enniskerry

Bollinger RD 2002
Champagne

TASTING NOTE
Expensive but magnificent Champagne, a superb complex combination of grilled nuts, citrus minerality, and subtle notes of honey and fruit.

DRINK WITH
Mushroom risotto, suggests Bollinger, but it is also a great aperitif.

STYLE
Sparkling

GRAPE VARIETY
Chardonnay, Pinot Noir

BACKSTORY
All major Champagne houses make a luxury Champagne. We are familiar with the names; Dom Perignon, Cristal, Krug, Bollinger RD, but sadly less familiar with the wines. They are all ridiculously expensive, the favoured tipple of the wealthy, rappers, rock stars, actors and business people alike. Much as I would love to dislike something so elitist and bling, on the rare occasions that I do get to taste them, I have to admit they are very, very good.

CRISP
REFRESHING WHITES

11

Santa Rita 120
Sauvignon Blanc
2014, Central Valley
Chile 13.5% **€11.99**

STOCKISTS: Widely available

Santa Rita 120 Sauvignon Blanc
2014 Central Valley

TASTING NOTE

The 2014, fresh on your shelves, is ultra-fresh with mouth-watering acidity and racy peach fruits.

DRINK WITH

A good all-purpose wine – as an aperitif or with lighter salads and fish.

STYLE

Crisp refreshing whites

GRAPE VARIETY

Sauvignon Blanc

BACKSTORY

If you think this wine is included because the brand is sponsoring the book, think again. This is Ireland's best-selling wine, and, at a recent tasting, the latest vintage showed really well against the competition- certainly great value at the price.

12 McWilliams Mount Pleasant
Eliza Semillon 2012, Hunter Valley
Australia 11% **€12**

McWILLIAM'S

MOUNT PLEASANT
ELIZA

McWilliam's Mount Pleasant Estate was established by legendary
winemaker Maurice O'Shea in 1921. Recognising qualities within his
wines that reflected the personalities of family and friends, their wines
continue a tradition of honouring these characters who shape our lives.

SEMILLON

2012 VINTAGE HUNTER VALLEY

STOCKISTS: Tesco

McWilliams Mount Pleasant
Eliza Semillon 2012, Hunter Valley

TASTING NOTE
Light and zippy with a floral nose and clean lemon fruits.

DRINK WITH
I would go for oysters, prawns or simply-cooked white fish.

STYLE
Crisp refreshing whites

GRAPE VARIETY
Semillon

BACKSTORY
Together the Hunter Valley and Semillon produce one of the greatest, most distinctive, white wines of Australia. Fresh and tangy with light lime and peach fruits when young, they develop delicious flavours of toasted nuts and woodsmoke within a few years. They last forever too. Tesco may still have a few bottles of the Mount Pleasant Elizabeth 2005, an aged version of the Eliza. Both are amazingly cheap - buy a bottle of each wine to see how Hunter Valley Semillon develops with age. A word of warning; Eliza is one of those promotional wines, sometimes priced at €19.99, only to be reduced to €10-12. Make sure you buy it at the lower price!

13 Domaine de Begude
Le Bel Ange 2013, IGP Pays d'Oc
France 12.5% **€12.99**

STOCKISTS: Supervalu

Domaine de Begude
Le Bel Ange 2013, IGP Pays d'Oc

TASTING NOTE

A perennial favourite. From a cool vineyard in Limoux, a marvellous, lip-smacking crisp dry white with clean green apple fruits.

DRINK WITH

James reckons it works best with oysters. But a good all-rounder to partner all things fishy.

STYLE

Crisp refreshing whites

GRAPE VARIETY

Chardonnay, Chenin Blanc

BACKSTORY

Englishman James Kinglake and his wife Catherine were working hard in London; Catherine was unable to conceive. They moved on to their second dream, a vineyard in France. Lo and behold a baby was born. Le Bel Ange. They now have the best of both worlds. The Limoux area, close to Carcassonne, produces some very good Chardonnay. Le Bel Ange always reminds me of a really good Chablis – at half the price.

14

Ziereisen Heugumber 2013
Badescher Landwein
Germany 11.5% **€14.95**

STOCKISTS: Clontarf Wines; Liston's; 64wine; Wicklow
Wine Co; Redmonds, Ranelagh

Ziereisen Heugumber 2013
Badescher Landwein

TASTING NOTE
Charming refreshing light pure pear fruits with a dry
finish. A perfect aperitif.

DRINK WITH
Friends – a bit too delicate to have with food; a talking
point to sip before dinner.

STYLE
Crisp refreshing whites

GRAPE VARIETY
Chasselas/Gutedel

BACKSTORY
You may not have come across Chasselas before but it is
widely grown in Switzerland and, in this case, just over the
border in Germany. The name may be unpronounceable to
English speakers, but it is worth the effort - this is one of
the finest examples of Chasseas I have tasted.

15 Sartarelli Verdicchio
dei Castelli di Jesi 2012
Italy 13% €15/£9.95

STOCKISTS: James Nicholson; www.jnwine.com

Sartarelli Verdicchio dei Castelli di Jesi 2012

TASTING NOTE
Plump pears and peaches backed up by mouth-watering fresh acidity.

DRINK WITH
Perfect with any simple seafood dishes..

STYLE
Crisp refreshing whites

GRAPE VARIETY
Verdicchio

BACKSTORY
Verdicchio can sometimes be fairly neutral; easy to drink but nothing to get excited about. In the right hands, and Sartarelli are the right hands, it can produce some beautifully rich yet refreshing dry whites.

16 Sauvignon Blanc Les Hautes Lieux 2013
Famille Bougrier, Vin de France
France 12% **€15.49**

STOCKISTS: O'Briens

Sauvignon Blanc Les Hautes Lieux 2013 Famille Bougrier, Vin de France

TASTING NOTE
Subtle floral aromas and fresh zesty clean green fruits, finishing dry.

DRINK WITH
Goats cheese or lighter salads.

STYLE
Crisp refreshing whites

GRAPE VARIETY
Sauvignon Blanc

BACKSTORY
Sauvignon Blanc from the Loire Valley tends to be a little lighter and less aromatic than those from New Zealand or Chile. This is not a bad thing in my book. They still have a wonderful zestiness and, in the better versions, a mouth-watering cleansing minerality.

17 Ktimi Kir-Yianni Petra 2013
PGI Macedonia
Greece 13% €15.99

STOCKISTS: On the Grapevine, Dalkey; Cabot & Co, Westport; The Corkscrew, Chatham Street; Listons, Camden Street; Jus de Vine, Portmarnock; Mortons, Galway; Red Island Wines, Skerries.

Ktimi Kir-Yianni Petra 2013
PGI Macedonia

TASTING NOTE
Ripe pear and pineapple fruits with an inviting fresh juicy character.

DRINK WITH
I consumed platefuls of the most beautiful, simply-cooked fish and seafood with this wine – octopus, calamari, prawns, and sea bass. Heavenly.

STYLE
Crisp refreshing whites

GRAPE VARIETY
Roditis Malagousia

BACKSTORY
I came across the wines of Ktimi Kir-Yianni in 2013, and was lucky enough to visit the estate earlier this year. The region is remote and beautiful, the wines original and compelling; each sip tastes different to the previous one. The red wine probably deserves a place in this book as well, but the white is the star here – a seamless mix of fruit and tangy freshness.

18 Jaspi Blanc 2012
Coca y Fito, Terra Alta
Spain 13.5% **€16.49**

STOCKISTS: O'Briens

Jaspi Blanc 2012
Coca y Fito, Terra Alta

TASTING NOTE
Bracing and herby with an inviting texture and a snappy dry finish.

DRINK WITH
Richer seafood dishes; perfect for a seafood risotto.

STYLE
Crisp refreshing whites

GRAPE VARIETY
Garnacha Blanca

BACKSTORY
Miquel and Toni Fitó, two brothers from Catalunya, are responsible for a string of superb original wines from the region. Toni makes the wine, Miquel designs the labels and sells the produce. The wines are great examples of the unique creativity and character that is Catalunya.

19

Geil Riesling Trocken
Rheinhessen 2013
Germany 12% **€16.50**

STOCKISTS: 64wine, Glasthule; Sweeneys, Glasnevin;
Clontarf Wines; plus many independent wine shops.

Geil Riesling Trocken
Rheinhessen 2013

TASTING NOTE
Free-flowing fresh and spritzy with delicate apple fruits.
Summer in a glass.

DRINK WITH
A wine to sip while preparing Friday night's dinner.

STYLE
Crisp refreshing whites

GRAPE VARIETY
Riesling

BACKSTORY
I love German Riesling; it has a wonderful combination of
snow-fresh lightness and subtle fruit. Sadly most fall into
the €20 plus price range. The Geil Riesling offers a great
introduction to the style at a very reasonable price.

20 Trimbach Riesling 2011
Alsace
France 12.5% **€18.99**

STOCKISTS: 64wine, Glasthule; Sweeneys, Glasnevin;
Clontarf Wines; plus many independent wine shops.

Trimbach Riesling 2011
Alsace

TASTING NOTE
Pure peach and green apple fruits balanced perfectly by
crisp citrus acidity. Great value.

DRINK WITH
Asian food, most fish dishes and chicken or pork.

STYLE
Crisp refreshing whites

GRAPE VARIETY
Riesling

BACKSTORY
One of two wines from Trimbach in this book. There are
very few producers who can combine size and quality, but
Trimbach wines are consistently good. Connoisseurs will
know the fabulous Clos St Hune and Frédéric Emile, but
this Riesling is terrific value for money.

21
Emrich-Schoenleber Riesling
Trocken 2012, Nahe
Germany 12.5% **€19.95**

STOCKISTS: Clontarf Wines; Liston's, Camden Street;
64wine, Glasthule; Searsons, Monkstown; La Touche,
Greystones; Power & Smullen, Lucan.

Emrich-Schoenleber Riesling
Trocken 2012, Nahe

TASTING NOTE
Light, slightly spritzy with cool, clean, lean green apple
fruits, finishing dry.

DRINK WITH
A herby crab salad or it also works as a magnificent
light aperitif.

STYLE
Crisp refreshing whites

GRAPE VARIETY
Riesling

BACKSTORY
Frank Schoenleber and his father are big names in
Germany. Although based in an area not noted for quality,
they have carved out an enviable reputation for exquisite
feather-light vivid Rieslings. When I can afford it, I buy the
top single-vineyard wines; otherwise I content myself with
this crystalline wine.

22

Pieropan
Soave Classico 2013
Italy 12% **€19.99**

STOCKISTS: 64wine, Glasthule; Donnybrook Fair; Jus de Vine, Portmarnock; Mortons, Ranelagh; On the Grapevine, Dalkey; Red Island, Skerries; Sweeney's, Glasnevin; Thomas Woodberry, Galway; Thomas, Foxrock; World Wide Wines, Waterford; thewineshop.

Pieropan
Soave Classico 2013

TASTING NOTE
Almond blossoms on the nose; light, elegant,
sophisticated crisp green fruits with excellent minerality.
A perennial favourite.

DRINK WITH
Seafood, light salads and pasta dishes.

STYLE
Crisp refreshing whites

GRAPE VARIETY
Garganega, Trebbiano di Soave

BACKSTORY
When Soave was seen as little more than a cheap party
white, Leonildo Pieropan was one of the few producers to
have the courage and determination to stay focused on
quality. It must have been difficult at times, but Pieropan,
with his two sons, is now recognised as the master of
Soave, with a range of exquisite refreshing wines.

23 Friulano San Pietro 2013
I Clivi, Friuli Colli Orientali
Italy 12% **€20**

STOCKISTS: 64wine, Glasthule; Clontarf Wines; Blackrock Wine Cellar: Ennis (SCR), World Wide Wines, Waterford.

Friulano San Pietro 2013
I Clivi, Friuli Colli Orientali

TASTING NOTE
A limpid, pristine precise wine of the highest quality.
Lively complex green fruits with a mineral core.

DRINK WITH
Plain fish dishes or as a very superior aperitif.

STYLE
Crisp refreshing whites

GRAPE VARIETY
Friulano

BACKSTORY
Ferdinando Zanusso produces tiny quantities of wine
from two ancient vineyards in Friuli in north-eastern Italy.
He is a modest man, happy to let the wines speak for
themselves, but full of information if you ask questions.
The wines are light in alcohol and body but never lack for
flavour.

24 Pithon-Paillé Anjou Blanc
Mozaik 2010
France 13% **€21.70**

STOCKISTS: Fallon & Byrne, Exchequer Street;
Redmonds, Ranelagh; Le Caveau, Kilkenny.

Pithon-Paillé Anjou Blanc
Mozaik 2010

TASTING NOTE
Exhilarating fresh nervy quince fruits with a lovely dry mineral finish.

DRINK WITH
Salmon

STYLE
Crisp refreshing whites

GRAPE VARIETY
Chenin Blanc

BACKSTORY
Chenin Blanc from the Loire Valley can be breathtaking. Every style is available; sparkling, dry, medium-dry and sweet. In their infancy they don't always shine but after a few years they start to develop the most amazing and wonderfully complex flavours. Jo Pithon is something of a legend in the Loire, one of the first to farm organically and then biodynamically. He joined forces with his stepson Joseph Paillé in 2008 to create one of the great names of the Loire Valley.

25

Gaia Assyrtiko 2013
Santorini
Greece 13% **€22.99**

STOCKISTS: O'Briens

Gaia Assyrtiko 2013
Santorini

TASTING NOTE
Exhilarating precise acidity with pristine green fruits.
Inspiring, thrilling wine.

DRINK WITH
Crustaceans or shellfish are good, but a rich stew of
squid, peppers and tomatoes was perfect.

STYLE
Crisp refreshing whites

54

GRAPE VARIETY
Assyrtiko

BACKSTORY
Most of us know Santorini as a tourist resort. However, it
is also home to some of the most unique wines. The local
Assyrtiko grape, trained into an intricate basket shape
to protect it from the winds, produces the most amazing
assertive dry wines, with a salty tang that is attributed to
the volcanic soils. It may not sound promising, but the
wines are bracing, fascinating and delicious.

26 Frantz Saumon Montlouis
Minérale+ 2012
France 12% **€23.20**

STOCKISTS: Baggot St. Wines; Clontarf Wines;
The Corkscrew, Chatham Street; World Wide Wines,
Waterford; Le Caveau, Kilkenny; 64wine, Glasthule;
Redmonds, Ranelagh; Fallon & Byrne, Exchequer Street.

Frantz Saumon Montlouis
Minérale+ 2012

TASTING NOTE
Exquisite, beautifully crafted thirst-quenching wine with
pristine orchard fruits, a touch of honey and beeswax and
a mouth-watering mineral tang.

DRINK WITH
Fish in a creamy sauce.

STYLE
Crisp refreshing whites

GRAPE VARIETY
Chenin blanc

BACKSTORY
Some of you will have heard the term natural wine. It is
not a precise category, having no definition, but covers a
diverse group of producers who work with as few additives
and treatments as possible. This includes Sulphur Dioxide,
without which it is very difficult to make a stable wine. It
is a highly controversial topic and has lead to very heated
debates - just google the term to see. Nobody will deny
that there are some great wines being made and this is
one. Franz Saumon came late to wine, having worked
as a forester in Quebec. He now runs a small vineyard in
Montlouis in the Loire Valley, fashioning a series of brilliant
wines from Chenin Blanc.

27

Jim Barry The Lodge Hill
Riesling 2013, Clare Valley
Australia 12.5% **€24.99**

JIM
BARRY

THE
LODGE HILL
DRY
RIESLING
2013

The
Lodge Hill
vineyard is one
of the highest in the
Clare Valley at 480m. The
altitude ensures cool nights
and warm days, producing grapes
with great flavour and elegance. 750ml

TROPHY GO

STOCKISTS: The Corkscrew, Chatham St; O'Briens.

Jim Barry The Lodge Hill
Riesling 2013, Clare Valley

TASTING NOTE
Clare Valley Riesling at its best; lifted aromatic nose, nuanced, light, clean, fresh green fruits with a long dry finish.

DRINK WITH
Perfection with crab salad but great with most seafood.

STYLE
Crisp refreshing whites

GRAPE VARIETY
Riesling

BACKSTORY
Peter Barry is the senior member of a famous clan of winemakers, and part of a diminishing group of pioneering wine producers who first put Australia on the world stage. They work hard and live hard too, happy to party whenever the opportunity arises. Barry always has a twinkle in his eye. This gang are generally very modest about their achievements. In the case of Barry, a little arrogance could be forgiven, as he is now heads up a very successful company that produces some of the finest wines of Australia. The most famous is Armagh, a massive Shiraz, but his Rieslings are the real bargain; reasonably priced and full of flavour.

28

Sancerre 2013
Domaine Paul Prieur
France 13% **€23-25**

STOCKISTS: Leopardstown Inn; Mortons, Ranelagh;
Molloys; Village O/L Castleknock, Thomas, Foxrock;
Callans, Dundalk.

Sancerre 2013
Domaine Paul Prieur

TASTING NOTE
Exquisite, fine, palate-tingling crisp green fruits with a
wonderful dry finish.

DRINK WITH
Seafood, white meats, goats cheese

STYLE
Crisp refreshing whites

GRAPE VARIETY
Sauvignon Blanc

BACKSTORY
Every wine shop has a Sancerre, usually well-made
but not terribly exciting. You sometimes forget just how
thrilling the best examples can be. A small group of the
region's producers continue to make some of the best dry
white wines around, razor-sharp, austere, mineral-laden
wines that express the true beauty of Sauvignon Blanc.

29 Keller von den Fels
Riesling 2012, Rheinhessen
Germany 12.5% **€32**

STOCKISTS: Cabot & Co, Westport; On The Grapevine, Dalkey

Keller von den Fels
Riesling 2012, Rheinhessen

TASTING NOTE
Superb, light, precise mineral and green fruits with wonderful length. A stunning wine, fresh, crisp with a delicious edge of clean but complex fruits. Mind-blowing stuff.

DRINK WITH
Crab dishes or as an aperitif

STYLE
Crisp refreshing whites

GRAPE VARIETY
Riesling

BACKSTORY
Still a young man, Klaus-Peter Keller is recognised as one of the finest winemakers in Germany. Self-confident, opinionated and talented, he crafts a series of brilliant wines in a region not always noted for quality. His sweet wines attract huge sums of money. However, his dry whites are also superb and more reasonably priced.

30
Trimbach Cuvée Frédéric Emile 2004
Riesling Alsace
France 12.5% **€43**

63

STOCKISTS: Mitchell & Son; Kellys Wine Vault;
Redmonds, Ranelagh; 64wine, Glasthule; Sweeneys,
Glasnevin; Jus de Vine, Portmarnock.

Trimbach Cuvée Frédéric Emile 2004
Riesling Alsace

TASTING NOTE

One of my favourite white wines vintage after vintage. Elegant and light in alcohol but with perfectly formed complex fruits, a hint of grilled nuts finishing with a flourish

DRINK WITH

Very good with fish, crab in particular, and chicken and pork dishes.

STYLE

Crisp refreshing whites

GRAPE VARIETY

Riesling

BACKSTORY

Despite being a relatively large operation, the Trimbach family consistently produces a series of very high-quality white wines. The single vineyard, Clos Sainte Hune, is one of the great wines of France. However, the basic Riesling and Cuvee Frédéric Emile, both of which appear in this book, offer exceptional value. The Frédéric Emile is from two Grand Cru vineyards, Osterberg and Gaisberg.

FRESH AND FRUITY

31

Roberta Fugatti
Pinot Grigio 2012, Trentino
Italy 12% **€13.50**

STOCKISTS: Sheridans Shops (Dublin, Galway,
Carnaross Co.Meath) plus online; Rua Deli, Castlebar;
Blackrock Cellar; The Wine Workshop, Dublin.

Roberta Fugatti
Pinot Grigio 2012, Trentino

TASTING NOTE
Vibrant, fresh, textured melon fruits with plenty of
life and zest.

DRINK WITH
Salads and fishy starters or as an aperitif

STYLE
Fresh and fruity

GRAPE VARIETY
Pinot Grigiio

BACKSTORY
With so much bland and tasteless Pinot Grigio around, it
was a pleasure to come across this wine from Trentino, in
the north of Italy, which restored my faith in the variety.

32 Quinta do Ribeiro Santo
2013, Dao
Portugal 13% €13.99

STOCKISTS: La Touche, Greystones; Fallon & Byrne;
Corkscrew; Deveney; Sweeney's; D Six; The Black Pig;
The Wine Shop, Perrystown, O'Donovans; Fresh.

Quinta do Ribeiro Santo 2013, Dao

TASTING NOTE
A blend of Encruzado and Malvasia Fina, this is
an appetising, vibrant, fresh white wine with clean
toothsome fruits.

DRINK WITH
A great all-rounder; serve on its own or with nibbles,
salads, fish and white meats.

STYLE
Fresh and fruity

GRAPE VARIETY
Encruzado, Malvasia

BACKSTORY
There are times when you look around for something
new to drink, but don't want to break the bank. Portugal
has a spellbinding array of local grapes, including many
white varieties. Over the last year, I have tasted a number
of really exciting white wines from various parts of the
country, often at very reasonable prices. Don't miss out.

33

**Simone Joseph
Chardonnay 2013**
Vin de pays d'Oc
France 13.5% **€13.99**

STOCKISTS: The Wine Store: www.thewinestore.ie; Jus de Vine, Portmarnock; The Vintry, Rathgar; Grapevine, Dalkey; Donnybrook Fair, The Drink Store, D7; Listons, Camden St.; Sweeneys, Glasnevin; Cases, Galway; The Vineyard, Galway.

Simone Joseph Chardonnay
2013 Vin de pays d'Oc

TASTING NOTE
Fresh, free-flowing, pure plump apple fruits - irresistible easy-drinking wine.

DRINK WITH
A good all-purpose crowd-pleasing wine that you can happily serve with all manner of fish, white meats and salads - perhaps even a buffet wine?

STYLE
Fresh and fruity

GRAPE VARIETY
Chardonnay

BACKSTORY
Simon and Emma Tyrrell make a formidable team, somehow managing to operate as winemakers, cidermakers, and wine importers servicing some of the country's best restaurants and wine shops. The Simone Joseph range of wines is impressive - balanced and full of clean fruits and at a great price.

34

Vina Laguna Malvazija 2013
Istria
Croatia 13% **€14.99**

STOCKISTS: Martins, Fairview; Mitchell & Son, IFSC & Sandycove; Wineonline.ie

Vina Laguna Malvazija 2013
Istria, Croatia

TASTING NOTE
Lightly aromatic with very appealing plump, honeyed, fresh melon fruits.

DRINK WITH
A good all-purpose wine to serve solo or with lighter salads, quiches and fish.

STYLE
Fresh and fruity

GRAPE VARIETY
Malvasia Istriana

BACKSTORY
I first tasted a range of fascinating Croatian wines five years ago. This is a country with a long tradition in winemaking and a range of unique grape varieties. Earlier this year, I was lucky enough to visit Istria and its beautiful coastline. The food was excellent, and the wines, made primarily from local varieties, were charming and accessible. In particular, wines made from their version of the Malvasia grape struck me as the perfect option for those who are tiring of Sauvignon Blanc - aromatic, fresh and fruity.

35

Monterrei
Terra de Lobo 2013
Spain 13.5% **€15.99**

STOCKISTS: Wines on the Green; Jus de Vine; The Black Pig; Blackrock Cellars; Cases; McCabes; Vintry; Hollands of Bray; Deveneys, Dundrum; Martins Off-licence; Dicey Reillys; Baggot Street Wines; Drinkstore

Monterrei
Terra de Lobo 2013

TASTING NOTE
Apricots and baked apples with hints of spice. Medium-bodied and full of fruit.

DRINK WITH
Richer seafood and fish dishes

STYLE
Fresh and fruity

GRAPE VARIETY
Godello

BACKSTORY
Monterrei is in Galicia, up in the north-west corner of Spain, right beside the Portuguese border. The wines are similar in style to those of Valdeorras and Rias Baixas - fresh and filled with juicy fruits.

36

Tahbilk Marsanne 2010
Victoria
Australia 12.5% **€16.70**

STOCKISTS: Wines Direct, Mullingar, www.winesdirect.ie

Tahbilk Marsanne 2010
Victoria

TASTING NOTE
Light toasted nut aromas, fresh textured pineapple fruits and excellent length. Great wine at a very reasonable price.

DRINK WITH
Prawns in something herby or slightly spicy.

STYLE
Fresh and fruity

GRAPE VARIETY
Marsanne

BACKSTORY
Tahbilk is one of the legendary estates of Australia producing some of the most long-lived and characterful wines. At first look, it does not appear a promising place to make white wine. The area around the Nagambie Lakes is dry and flat. Yet alongside a wonderfully deep leathery Shiraz, Tahbilk produces very good Viognier and some brilliant age-worthy Marsanne at a very reasonable price.

37

Amalaya Torrontés
Riesling 2014, Cafayate
Argentina 13.5% **€16.99**

STOCKISTS: World Wide Wines, Waterford; Donnybrook
Fair; Redmonds, Ranelagh.

Amalaya Torrontés
Riesling 2014, Cafayate

TASTING NOTE
One of my favourite white wines, free-flowing and fresh with vibrant pineapple and orange fruits.

DRINK WITH
Salads and white meats or as a very agreeable fruit-filled aperitif.

STYLE
Fresh and fruity

GRAPE VARIETY
Torrontés Riesling

BACKSTORY
This is the little brother of the Colomé Malbec, also featured in this book. Amalaya is in the Calchaqui Valley, in the north of Argentina. This is one of the highest wine-growing regions in the world, and the white wines retain a wonderful natural acidity that combines beautifully with the ripe fruit. Torrontés originated in Galicia in Spain, but is widely grown in Argentina. This is one of the finest versions I have come across.

38

Mâcon-Uchizy
Domaine Talmard 2013
France 13.5% **€16.99**

Mâcon-Uchizy

APPELLATION CONTROLÉE

2013

MIS EN BOUTEILLE À LA PROPRIÉTÉ PAR

Mallory & Benjamin Talmard
Propriétaires-Récoltants à Uchizy, Saône-&-Loire, France

VIN BLANC – WHITE WINE – PRODUIT DE FRANCE – PRODUCE OF FRANCE

STOCKISTS: Jus de Vine, Portmarnock; The Drink Store, Manor St; 64wine, Glasthule; Cases, Galway; The Wine Room @ One Pery Square.

Mâcon-Uchizy
Domaine Talmard 2013

TASTING NOTE
Light, fresh, racy Chardonnay with succulent juicy plump apple fruits.

DRINK WITH
Most white fish, salmon and chicken dishes.

STYLE
Fresh and fruity

GRAPE VARIETY
Chardonnay

BACKSTORY
In addition to the inexpensive but slightly dull Mâcon-Lugny, the Mâconnais produces some of the best-value white wines of Burgundy. The best known names are Pouilly-Fuissé and Saint Véran, but there are 26 other villages that go under the name Mâcon-Villages and a handful entitled to use their own village name. The region has no shortage of ambitious talented growers who offer their wines at very reasonable prices. Some are made in a rich honeyed style, others, such as this example, are crisp and dry.

39

José Pariente
Rueda Verdejo 2013
Spain 13% **€17.15**

STOCKISTS: Wines Direct, Mullingar www.winesdirect.ie

José Pariente
Rueda Verdejo 2013

TASTING NOTE
Fresh, tangy, lemon and grapefruit, balanced out by
clean green fruits, and a dry finish.

DRINK WITH
All things fishy or by itself.

STYLE
Fresh and fruity

GRAPE VARIETY
Verdejo

BACKSTORY
A house wine in El Bulli for four years, this is one of the
finest examples of Rueda, and a wine to win over Sauvignon
drinkers. The Verdejo grape is a local speciality, aromatic
and forward, with zesty crisp fruits.

40 Ribeiro Eira dos Mouros
Casal de Arman 2013
Spain 13% **€17.65**

EIRA DOS MOUROS

RIBEIRO
DENOMINACIÓN DE ORIGEN

Product of Spain

STOCKISTS: Searsons, Monkstown; Jus de Vine,
Portmarnock.

Ribeiro Eira dos Mouros
Casal de Arman 2013

TASTING NOTE
Luscious, fresh, exotic fruits kept nicely in check by a
bracing acidity, finishing bone dry.

DRINK WITH
Locally, octopus salad with pimento, but any shellfish
would do nicely.

STYLE
Fresh and fruity

GRAPE VARIETY
Treixadura, Godello, Albariño, Loureira, Caino Blanco,
Torrontés

BACKSTORY
Galicia, right up in the north-west corner of Spain produces
its share of delicious fresh fruit-filled white wines. We are
more familiar with Rías Baixas, from the coastal region, but
several areas further inland are responsible for some of the
most exciting wines. The grape varieties are unfamiliar and
difficult to pronounce, but the wines are great. Look out for
the wines of Valdeorras, Monterrei and Ribeira.

41 Chardonnay 2012,
Terres Dorées,
Jean-Paul Brun, Beaujolais Blanc
France 12% **€17.95**

87

STOCKISTS: Wines Direct, Mullingar www.winesdirect.ie

Chardonnay 2012, Terres Dorées

Jean-Paul Brun, Beaujolais Blanc

TASTING NOTE

A subtle and delectable blend of citrus and green fruits with a touch of honey.

DRINK WITH

An amazing aperitif or posh party wine, although it would also partner nicely with lighter fish dishes.

STYLE

Fresh and fruity

GRAPE VARIETY

Chardonnay

BACKSTORY

There are times when less is more. Jean Paul Brun makes wines with less alcohol and no new oak. The result is a series of sublime elegant red and white wines that refresh and satisfy without having to try. One of the few white few Beaujolais available in Ireland.

42 Soalheiro Alvarinho 2013
Vinho Verde
Portugal 12.5% **€18.49/£13.50**

STOCKISTS: James Nicholson, Crossgar, jnwine.com

Soalheiro Alvarinho 2013
Vinho Verde

TASTING NOTE
An excellent, refined light wine with succulent pure clean green fruits and a lovely long dry finish.

DRINK WITH
Fish and shellfish

STYLE
Fresh and fruity

GRAPE VARIETY
Alvarinho

BACKSTORY
A tasting of Portuguese Vinho Verdes from the Minho region last year changed my mind about these wines. In the past, producers were happy to knock out very light, slightly fizzy wines that were sometimes disconcertingly sweet. But just across the border, Galicia has been producing wonderful fruit-filled wines largely using the Albariño grape. And now Portugal has started to do the same. Some of the wines are lighter, but in overall quality, these are every bit as good if not better, than their Spanish counterparts.

43 Bründlmayer Riesling
Kamptaler Terrassen
Austria 13% **€19.95**

91

STOCKISTS: Greenacres, Wexford

Bründlmayer Riesling
Kamptaler Terrassen

TASTING NOTE
A sophisticated racy wine with lively refreshing citrus and green fruits and a long, dry mineral finish.

DRINK WITH
With fish, chicken and pork dishes. Also a perfect aperitif.

STYLE
Fresh and fruity

GRAPE VARIETY
Riesling

BACKSTORY
Willi Bründlmayer is one of Austria's greatest winemakers. He produces a string of wines, some very good, others brilliant. A visit to the Bründlmayer stand at a wine fair takes time, but is always worth it. The range is breathtaking - red wines, an excellent sparkling wine, as well as Chardonnay, Pinot Blanc and Pinot Gris. But the highlights are always to be found amongst the Rieslings and Grüner Veltliners, a series of breathtaking, complex, lingering wines, each echoing the vineyards from which they sprung. We are lucky to have the Bründlmayer wines available in Ireland again after a few years absence.

44

Lagar de Costa Albariño
Rias Baixas 2013
Spain 13% **€19.99**

STOCKISTS: O'Briens

Lagar de Costa Albariño
Rias Baixas 2013

TASTING NOTE
Succulent plump pear fruits with a lively
zesty lemon edge.

DRINK WITH
Good served solo, but the locals would go for a plate of
mixed shellfish, simply served with wedges of lemon.

STYLE
Fresh and fruity

GRAPE VARIETY
Albariño

BACKSTORY
A look at Lagar de Costa is to see how Rías Baixas has
changed with increased popularity. Where once grapes
were supplied to a single large local producer, now the
smaller estates make their own wine. Lagar de Costa has
six hectares of Albariño, with some vines over 50 years
old. From this they fashion small quantities of high-quality
wines. Like many in the area, they also have refurbished
accommodation available to rent.

45

Louro do Bolo
Valdeorras 2013
Spain 13.5% **€22**

STOCKISTS: Black Pig, Donnybrook; 64wine, Glasthule;
On the Grapevine, Dalkey; The Corkscrew, Chatham St.;
Jus de Vine, Portmarnock; The Wine Work Shop, Baggot
St.Red Island, Skerries; Clontarf Wines; The Wicklow Wine Co.

Louro do Bolo
Valdeorras 2013

TASTING NOTE
Richly fruity with peaches and pears, wrapped around a
solid core of zingy acidity.

DRINK WITH
All kinds of fish and seafood.

STYLE
Fresh and fruity

GRAPE VARIETY
Godello

BACKSTORY
I was surprised when I saw how many white wines from
Galicia were included in this book, but they are currently
amongst my favourite wines. In style they are medium-
bodied, with plenty of mouth-watering fruit and no oak
flavours. Louro de Bolo is made by Rafael Palacios,
brother of Alvaro, one of the superstars of Spanish
winemaking. I can certainly recommend this wine, but if
you want to spoil yourself, go for the As Sortes, the top
wine of the estate. It is sensationally good.

46

O Rosal Terras Guada
Rias Baixas Albariño 2013
Spain 12% **€26**

STOCKISTS: The Wine Boutique, D4; Mannings, Ballylickey
Co Cork; Sweeney's, Glasnevin; Stacks, Co Kerry; Redmonds,
Ranelagh; Mitchell & Son, IFSC & Sandycove; Jus de Vine.
Portmarnock; The Market D18; Matsons, Bandon.

O Rosal Terras Guada
Rias Baixas Albarinño 2013

TASTING NOTE
Ripe melon and white fruits cut through with zesty acidity
and excellent length.

DRINK WITH
A plate of plain shellfish for the best result but goes with
fish of all kinds.

STYLE
Fresh and fruity

GRAPE VARIETY
Albariño

BACKSTORY
An exemplar of the new breed of Spanish white wines.
Made with local grape varieties and full of interesting
flavours, these wines are taking Ireland, and the world,
by storm. Year after year, the O Rosal is up there with my
favourite white wines.

47 Schloss Gobelsburg
Grüner Veltliner Lamm
Reserve 2011, Kamptal
Austria 13.5% €30

STOCKISTS: Corkscrew, Chatham St.; Redmonds, Ranelagh;
Sweeneys, Glasnevin; Wicklow Wine Co.

Schloss Gobelsburg
Grüner Veltliner
Lamm Reserve 2011, Kamptal

TASTING NOTE
Rich, textured fruits and ginger countered by a lovely
refreshing acidity and a lingering dry finish.

DRINK WITH
Grüner Veltliner goes very well with Indian food –
try it with a prawn curry.

STYLE
Fresh and fruity

GRAPE VARIETY
Grüner Veltliner

BACKSTORY
Schloss Gobelsurg is an old castle run by the Cisterican
order. Included in its holdings are some of the finest
vineyards of Kamptal. Michael Moosbrugger has been
manager here since 1996. Over the last decade his wines
have improved greatly and are now ranked amongst the
very best in Austria. The entry-level (at around €15) is
delicious; this wine is sublime.

48 Greywacke Wild Sauvignon
Marlborough 2012
New Zealand 13% **€32.99**

GREYWACKE

WILD SAUVIGNON
MARLBOROUGH   NEW ZEALAND
2012

STOCKISTS: Jus de Vine, Portmarnock; Redmonds,
Ranelagh; The Corkscrew, Chatham St.; 64wine, Glasthule;
Blackrock Cellar; Clontarf Wines; Greenacres, Wexford;

Greywacke Wild Sauvignon
Marlborough 2012

TASTING NOTE
Marlborough Sauvignon with a difference - ripe peaches,
subtle nuts and a lovely complex finish.

DRINK WITH
Fish and shellfish

STYLE
Fresh and fruity

GRAPE VARIETY
Sauvignon Blanc

BACKSTORY
Kevin Judd is one of the legends of winemaking in New
Zealand, although you would never know it to meet him.
He is quiet and reserved, only becoming excited when he
talks about photography (his other passion in life) and
wine. As winemaker at Cloudy Bay, he helped bring worldwide fame to the Marlborough region. Greywacke is his
own winery, where he tries to make wines that offer more
interest than the standard Marlborough Sauvignon Blanc.

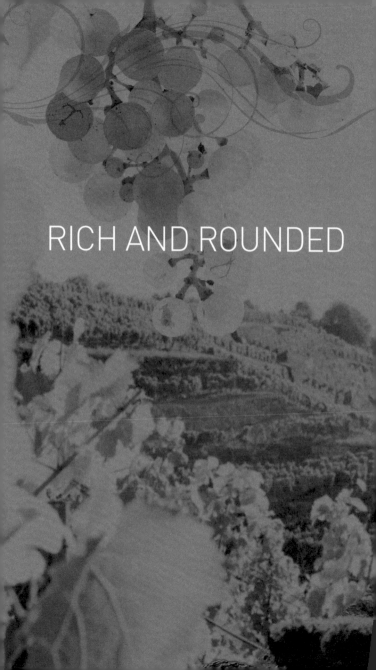

RICH AND ROUNDED

49

Les Auzines Fleurs Blanches
2013, Vin de France
France 12.5% **€14.49**

STOCKISTS: O'Briens

Les Auzines Fleurs Blanches
2013, Vin de France

TASTING NOTE
Lightly toasted notes combined with peaches, almonds and honey. Unusual and perfectly formed.

DRINK WITH
Rich seafood or chicken stews.

STYLE
Rich and rounded

GRAPE VARIETY
Grenache Gris

BACKSTORY
Laurent Miquel and his Irish wife Neasa Corish make an astonishingly wide range of wines from the Languedoc, many available in Ireland. Somehow they manage to keep the standards high across the board. This wine is from their most recent acquisition, a vineyard perched high up in the mountains in Corbières that they farm organically.

50

Cuvée des Conti
Tour des Gendres 2012, Bergerac
France 13.5% **€16**

STOCKISTS: Le Caveau, Kilkenny, lecaveau.ie ; Corkscrew,
Chatham St: thecorkscrew.ie; World Wide Wines, Waterford

Cuvée des Conti
Tour des Gendres 2012, Bergerac

TASTING NOTE
Made from 70% Semillon, this is a beautifully balanced
wine with zesty acidity and delicious rounded peach and
orange fruits.

DRINK WITH
Seafood, white meats

STYLE
Rich and rounded

GRAPE VARIETY
Semillon, Sauvignon

BACKSTORY
Bergerac is next door to Bordeaux, the world's most
famous vineyard. Not having a well-known name can be
a serious disadvantage when it comes to selling wine. It
means that you need to produce better wines at cheaper
prices. As a result, Bergerac can offer excellent value
for money. This wine blew me away at a recent tasting. I
wasn't surprised as Luc de Conti is one of my favourite
producers.

51 Santa Rita Medalla Real
Leyda Valley
Chardonnay 2011
Chile 13.9% **€19.99**

STOCKISTS: Widely available including Tesco, O'Donovans

Santa Rita Medalla Real
Leyda Valley Chardonnay 2011

TASTING NOTE
Restrained peach and apple fruits with subtle toasted nuts and a core of citrus acidity.

DRINK WITH
Fish, chicken, turkey dishes

STYLE
Rich and rounded

GRAPE VARIETY
Chardonnay

BACKSTORY
I am not a fan of new oak, but every now and again you find an example where it is used in an intelligent, understated way, and thus adds an extra layer of complexity. This is one such instance. If you think you don't like Chardonnay, I would suggest you try this out for size. The Leyda Valley, mentioned elsewhere in this book, is responsible for some of the most exciting wines coming out of Chile at the moment.

52 Domaine Sainte Rose
Roussanne 2011 VdP Oc
France 14% **€20.49/£13.75**

BARREL SELECTION
ROUSSANNE 2011

Domaine
Sainte Rose

STOCKISTS: James Nicholson, Crossgar jnwine.com

Domaine Sainte Rose
Roussanne 2011 VdP Oc

TASTING NOTE
A marvellous complex mix of rich creamy exotic fruits and subtle toasted nuts kept in check by a fine vein of acidity.

DRINK WITH
Richer fish dishes, chicken or turkey.

STYLE
Rich and rounded

GRAPE VARIETY
Roussanne

BACKSTORY
Charles Simpson was born in Ireland but moved to England at the age of four. He and his Scottish wife Ruth both gave up successful careers to set up Domaine Sainte Rose in the Languedoc. They enlisted the support of "twelve apostles", business people from the north and south of Ireland, and 12 years on, they have built a reputation for quality and innovation in an area more noted for tradition and volume production. Not content with that, the Simpsons have now bought a new site close to the Kent coast in England.

53

Miro Pinot Blanc 2012
Stajerska
Slovenia 13.5% **€22.50**

STOCKISTS: Cabot & Co, Westport;
On The Grapevine, Dalkey

Miro Pinot Blanc 2012
Stajerska

TASTING NOTE
Very appealing, textured, spicy melon fruits with plenty of
juicy acidity to keep it in check.

DRINK WITH
Richer fish dishes; try it with Thai curries.

STYLE
Rich and rounded

GRAPE VARIETY
Pinot Blanc

BACKSTORY
Slovenia produces some mouth-wateringly good white
wines - we just don't see them very often in this country.
Miro Munda is based in the east of the country; he
inherited some vines from his father and quickly moved
from making traditional inexpensive wines with little
flavour to a series of very good fruit-driven wines with real
character.

54

Ovilos 2012
Ktima Biblia Chora, Macedonia
Greece 14% **€23.99**

STOCKISTS: Baggot Street Wines; Redmonds, Ranelagh;
McCabes; Wines on the Green; Donnybrook Fair; Cases,
Galway; Gibneys, Malahide; Hollands, Bray; Jus de Vine,
Portmarnock

Ovilos 2012
Ktima Biblia Chora, Macedonia

TASTING NOTE
A seductive, textured, toasty wine with mouth-watering apricots and peaches shot through with lime zest.

DRINK WITH
Salmon, scallops or lobster for a real treat.

STYLE
Rich and rounded

GRAPE VARIETY
Semillon, Assyrtiko

BACKSTORY
I tasted some great white wines from Greece this year and Ovilos was one of the best. Made by one of the country's leading winemakers, this unique blend of Semillon and the local specialty, Assyrtiko, was fermented in oak barrels This usually turns me off. However, it really works here. You can enjoy this now, but I tasted a few older vintages recently and it ages beautifully.

55

Springfield Wild Yeast
Chardonnay 2012, Robertson
South Africa 14% **€25**

STOCKISTS: Jus De Vine, Portmarnock; The Parting Glass,
Enniskerry; Matsons, Grange; No 21, Midleton

Springfield Wild Yeast
Chardonnay 2012, Robertson

TASTING NOTE
Overflowing with delectable rich apple and peach fruits,
complemented by a subtle but persistent mineral acidity.

DRINK WITH
Pumpkin risotto, salmon

STYLE
Rich and rounded

GRAPE VARIETY
Chardonnay

BACKSTORY
Jeanette Bruwer always has something new up her sleeve
when she visits Ireland, usually involving some crazy
winemaking scheme with her brother Abrie Bruwer. The
results speak for themselves though; a string of delicious
aromatic Sauvignons, some restrained, elegant red wines,
and one of my all-time favourite New World Chardonnays.

56

Bernhard Ott Fass4
Grüner Veltliner 2013
Austria 13% **€27**

STOCKISTS: 64wine, Glasthule; Clontarf Wines.

Bernhard Ott Fass4
Grüner Veltliner 2013

TASTING NOTE
An exuberant, fresh wine bursting with pineapples and
tropical fruits.

DRINK WITH
Creamy fish and chicken dishes including Asian curries.

STYLE
Rich and rounded

GRAPE VARIETY
Grüner Veltliner

BACKSTORY
I came across these guys at a fair in Austria this year;
there was a crowd around the table, always a good sign.
The wines simply exploded with flavour and lingered
beautifully. Break open the piggy bank.

57

Shaw & Smith
M3 Chardonnay 2013,
Adelaide Hills
Australia 12.5% **€34.99**

SHAW + SMITH

M3 Chardonnay
Adelaide Hills
2013

STOCKISTS: La Touche, Greystones; Redmond's, Ranelagh;
Mitchell & Son, IFSC & Glasthule; The Corkscrew, Chatham St.

Shaw & Smith
M3 Chardonnay 2013, Adelaide Hills

TASTING NOTE
Elegant, crisp green apple fruits, with a vivid streak of
lemon zest, subtle toasty oak, and a long dry finish.

DRINK WITH
Grilled black sole with lots of butter.

STYLE
Rich and rounded

GRAPE VARIETY
Chardonnay

BACKSTORY
Australia is producing some top-notch Chardonnay
these days, and not in the big buttery style of old. The
Shaw & Smith version, from cool climate vineyards in the
Adelaide Hills, has more in common with the great wines
of Burgundy. In the recent past, I have aged a couple of
bottles for a year or two with great success.

LIGHT AND ELEGANT

58

Horizon de Lynch 2011
Médoc
France 12.5% **€12.50**

GRAND VIN DE BORDEAUX

HORIZON DE LYNCH

MÉDOC
APPELLATION MÉDOC CONTRÔLÉE

— 2011 —

MIS EN BOUTEILLE À P. 33450
PAR BORIE-MANOUX À BORDEAUX - FRANCE
PRODUCT OF FRANCE · PRODUIT DE FRANCE

12.5%vol.   75cl

STOCKISTS: Dunnes Stores

Horizon de Lynch 2011
Médoc

TASTING NOTE
Classic Médoc with light, restrained, blackcurrant fruits and a smooth dry finish.

DRINK WITH
A plain roast of lamb or beef - Sunday lunch

STYLE
Light and elegant

GRAPE VARIETY
Merlot, Cabernet Sauvignon

BACKSTORY
Inexpensive Bordeaux can be a bit of a lottery; there is no shortage of weedy acidic wine. However, the good versions make for very satisfying drinking with their subtle elegant fruits and drying tannins on the finish. Bordeaux should never be big, rich and ripe; it is all about subtlety and restrained, less being more.

59

Jean Colin Pinot Noir 2013
Vin de France
France 12.5% **€12.99**

127

STOCKISTS: Donnybrook Fair

Jean Colin Pinot Noir 2013
Vin de France

TASTING NOTE
Fragrant light Pinot with vibrant lifted redcurrant and red cherry fruits.

DRINK WITH
Pork and charcuterie or by itself.

STYLE
Light and elegant

GRAPE VARIETY
Pinot Noir

BACKSTORY
It says Vin de France, but I suspect that the grapes come from the Loire Valley, as Jean Colin is based in Thauvenay in Sancerre. This is a very tasty, light, fresh red with crunchy redcurrant and red cherry fruits. It has good acidity making it a perfect foil for pork dishes and charcuterie in particular. It is rare to find a decent French Pinot for under €20, let alone €15, so this is something of a bargain. It is imported directly by Donnybrook Fair.

60

Ch. Bellevue La Forêt 2010
Fronton
France 13.5% **€14.99**

STOCKISTS: Molloys; Next Door, nationwide; The Vintry, Rathgar; Thomas's Foxrock; Florries, Tramore; Paul's Donegal

Ch. Bellevue La Forêt 2010
Fronton

TASTING NOTE
Delicious vibrant red cherry fruits with a twist of black pepper.

DRINK WITH
Cold meats, sausages

STYLE
Light and elegant

GRAPE VARIETY
Negrette, Syrah, Cabernet Franc, Cabernet Sauvignon

BACKSTORY
This property has been owned by Irishman Phillip Grant since 2008. Fronton is a large region to the north of Toulouse that produces some very under-rated wines. The local speciality is the Negrette grape, which has been around since time immemorial. The best wines are fragrant with a vivid fruitiness and a nice bite to the finish. Great wines for lighter red and white meat dishes, or a plate of firm cheeses. As you may have guessed, I am a big fan.

61

Carmen Right Wave
Leyda Valley Pinot Noir 2013
Chile 13.5% **€14.99**

STOCKISTS: Widely available including Dunnes, SuperValu,
Eurospar and Tesco.

Carmen Right Wave
Leyda Valley Pinot Noir 2013

TASTING NOTE
Light, easy-drinking wine with very moreish red juicy cherry fruits.

DRINK WITH
A good multi-purpose wine that you could serve by itself at a party, or with salmon or tuna, or a great many salads and white meat dishes.

STYLE
Light and elegant

GRAPE VARIETY
Pinot Noir

BACKSTORY
Chile has been creating some serious Pinot Noir in the Casablanca and Leyda Valleys for some time now. The fog rolling in from the Pacific keeps temperatures down (bring a geansaí if you visit) in these coastal regions, making it ideal for growing Sauvignon Blanc and Pinot Noir. If you like New Zealand Pinot then this is certainly worth checking out.

62

Stefano Accordini
Valpolicella Classico 2013
Italy 12.5% **€15.35**

Stefano Accordini
Valpolicella Classico 2013

TASTING NOTE
Light and juicy with plump plum and dark cherry fruits.

DRINK WITH
Pizzas and light pasta dishes.

STYLE
Light and elegant

GRAPE VARIETY
Corvina Rondinella

BACKSTORY
I have listed two Valpols in this book; they are such versatile wines, easy to sip on their own, but equally at home with a variety of foods. Pretty good with a mixed plate of charcuterie and cheese. Ripasso, a super-charged version of Valpolicella, seems to be all the rage currently, but I often prefer the vivid bright fruits of the less expensive 'basic' Valpol.

63

Ch. Sainte Marie 2012
Bordeaux Supérieur
France 13.5% **€15.75**

Ch. Sainte Marie 2012
Bordeaux Supérieur

TASTING NOTE
A delicious modern style of Bordeaux with light creamy cassis fruits and a smooth easy finish.

DRINK WITH
Roast beef or lamb

STYLE
Light and elegant

GRAPE VARIETY
Merlot, Cabernet Franc

BACKSTORY
Bordeaux produces a fair amount of thin, weedy inexpensive wines. We know all about the great wines, but these days can rarely afford to buy them. If you look hard, however, you can find that wonderful thing; a well-made, elegant, slightly aristocratic Bordeaux at a reasonable price. This is one such example.

64

Tenuta Cocci Grifoni
Le Torri 2010, Rosso
Piceno Superiore
Italy 13% **€15.95**

137

STOCKISTS: Coach House, Ballinteer; Michael's Wines,
Woodpark; Nectar, Sandyford; Probus Wines, Fenian St;
Terroirs, Donnybrook; The Wicklow Wine Co

Tenuta Cocci Grifoni
Le Torri 2010, Rosso Piceno Superiore

TASTING NOTE
Attractive, slightly rustic, juicy, brambly red fruits with
a nice bite.

DRINK WITH
Medium-bodied red and white meat dishes

STYLE
Light and elegant

GRAPE VARIETY
Montepulciano, Sangiovese

BACKSTORY
The Marches, on the eastern coast of central Italy,
produces an interesting range of fresh, crisp white wines
and toothsome lightly fruity reds. Most are very reasonably
priced and most go very well with medium-bodied foods.
As such this is one of my go-to regions for wines for mid-
week dinners.

65 **Domaine du Vissoux**
Beaujolais Cuvée
Traditionelle 2013
France 12% **€16.95**

PIERRE-MARIE CHERMETTE
Vissoux

Cuvée traditionnelle
Beaujolais vieilles vignes
APPELLATION BEAUJOLAIS CONTRÔLÉE

2 0 1 3

STOCKISTS: Terroirs, Donnybrook

Domaine du Vissoux
Beaujolais Cuvée Traditionelle 2013

TASTING NOTE
The lightest, most refreshing Beaujolais with succulent juicy strawberry and redcurrant fruits.

DRINK WITH
Terrines, patés and sausages

STYLE
Light and elegant

GRAPE VARIETY
Gamay

BACKSTORY
Domaine du Vissoux produces a string of wonderfully pure silky wines from the Beaujolais region. Its Fleurie is a delight, and its Moulin-a-Vent a serious age-worthy wine. But I love their basic basic Beaujolais Cuvée Traditionelle, a delightful lively vin du soif

66

Sipp Mack
Rosé d'Alsace 2013
France 13% **€17.49**

STOCKISTS: Mitchell & Son, CHQ, IFSC & Glasthule,
www.mitchellandson.com.

Sipp Mack
Rosé d'Alsace 2013

TASTING NOTE
Delightful, elegant, fragrant, raspberry-scented rosé.

DRINK WITH
Perfect for sipping on its own.

STYLE
Light and elegant

GRAPE VARIETY
Pinot Noir

BACKSTORY
This is the only rosé in the book. It is not that I dislike them, but, like many of you, I only start thinking about them when the sun comes out. However, the Sipp Mack rosé, which I tried again on a wet September evening, is worth drinking all year round. Alsace sometimes struggles to ripen Pinot Noir; perhaps more producers should concentrate on producing rosés such as this.

67

Geil Pinot Noir
Trocken 2012, Rheinhessen
Germany 13% **€17.50**

STOCKISTS: Sweeney's, Glasnevin; Clontarf Wines; Wicklow
Wine Co; Corkscrew, Chatham St; Blackrock Cellar

Geil Pinot Noir
Trocken 2012, Rheinhessen

TASTING NOTE
Charming, light, refreshing red cherry fruits.

DRINK WITH
Tuna or salmon or lighter pork dishes. Also perfect
on its own.

STYLE
Light and elegant

GRAPE VARIETY
Pinot Noir

BACKSTORY
Finding inexpensive Pinot Noir is not easy. This variety has
a reputation for behaving like a teenager - very stubborn
and difficult, wherever it is grown. Low yields are the
order of the day, meaning prices tend to be very steep.
However, a few countries manage to produce good Pinot
Noir at a reasonable price. This is one of my favourite
examples.

68

La Lippa 2012
Barbera d'Asti
Italy 13.5% **€17.50**

STOCKISTS: Coach House, Ballinteer; The Corkscrew, Chatham St; Coolers, Swords; Drinks Direct, Harolds Cross; Hole in the Wall, D7; Probus Wines, Fenian St; Silver Granite, Palmerstown; the Wicklow Wine Co

La Lippa 2012
Barbera d'Asti

TASTING NOTE
A lovely light, refreshing wine with moreish dark cherry fruits.

DRINK WITH
Mushroom risotto

STYLE
Light and elegant

146

GRAPE VARIETY
Barbera

BACKSTORY
Barbera will always play second fiddle to Nebbiolo, the great grape of Piemonte. However, from a good producer, you can come across some deliciously fresh, fruity, medium-bodied wines made with Barbera. And they are usually more affordably priced too.

69

Fp by Filipa Pato
'Lost in Translation' 2012,
Beira Atlantico
Portugal 12% **€18**

STOCKISTS: Clontarf Wines; 64 Wine; Blackrock Cellar;
The Drinkstore

Fp by Filipa Pato
'Lost in Translation' 2012, Beira Atlantico

TASTING NOTE
Delicious, tangy, fresh, cool, savoury dark cherry fruits
with a bitter twist and light tannins.

DRINK WITH
Ham, pork and lighter chicken dishes.

STYLE
Light and elegant

GRAPE VARIETY
Baga

BACKSTORY
Filipa Pato is the daughter of Luis Pato, one of Portugal's
foremost wine producers. Having cut her teeth in
Argentina, Bordeaux and Australia she returned home.
But instead of joining the family business, she began
renting vineyards to create her own wines. She has,
however, inherited her father's love of traditional
Portuguese grape varieties. Using these, she has
fashioned a series of quirky, free-flowing fresh wines that
are a joy to drink.

70

Fleurie
Domaine de la Madone 2012
France 13% **€18.49**

STOCKISTS: Mitchell & Son, CHQ, IFSC & Glasthule: mitchellandson.com; Myles Doyle's, Gorey; Anderson's Food Store, Glasnevin; Dicey Reilly's, Ballyshannon; Cases Wine Warehouse, Galway; The Wine Workshop, Leeson St

Fleurie
Domaine de la Madone 2012

TASTING NOTE
Wonderful fresh aromas and concentrated but light juicy strawberry fruits, with a lip-smacking lingering finish.

DRINK WITH
This is a light wine (13% alcohol and no tannins) so you could drink without food, but I would recommend it with anything porky, especially charcuterie, or chicken. I rarely drink wine during the day, but this would fit into that wonderful category of "luncheon wine".

150

STYLE
Light and elegant

GRAPE VARIETY
Gamay

BACKSTORY
I love good Beaujolais but these days the best wines all seem to cost more than €20. I was therefore delighted to come across this delicious Fleurie at a more affordable price.

71

Treinta Mil Maravedias
Bodega Marañones 2012,
DO Madrid
Spain 14% **€20**

STOCKISTS: Fallon & Byrne, Exchequer Street; Clontarf
Wines; 64wine, Glasthule; Blackrock Cellar; The Drinkstore,
D7; The Cheese Pantry, Drumcondra; Baggot Street Wines;
The Black Pig, Donnybrook; Red Island Wines, Skerries.

Treinta Mil Maravedias
Bodega Marañones 2012, DO Madrid

TASTING NOTE
A wonderful lifted fragrance of roses followed up by a
supremely elegant palate of strawberries and herbs.

DRINK WITH
Plainly grilled lamb

STYLE
Light and elegant

GRAPE VARIETY
Garnacha, Syrah

BACKSTORY
Fernando García Alonso is one of a number of young
winemakers who gravitated to the mountains south of
Madrid where they have revived the ancient wines of the
region with spectacular success. Using old Garnacha
vines, Fernando produces a series of superb elegant wines
that have a unique delicacy and finesse.

72

Moric Blaufränkisch
2012, Burgenland
Austria 13% **€22.99**

2012
**BLAU
FRÄNKISCH**
BURGENLAND
ÖSTERREICH QUALITÄTSWEIN TROCKEN
MIT STAATLICHER PRÜFNUMMER L-N 8305/13
PRODUZIERT UND ABGEFÜLLT VON ROLAND VELICH GMBH, A-7051 GROSSHÖFLEIN
ENTHÄLT SULFITE/CONTAINS SULFITES
WWW.MORIC.AT
13%VOL   750 ML
MORIC

STOCKISTS: On the Grapevine, Dalkey; Cabot & Co, Westport;
Market 57, Westport; 64wine, Glasthule; No 1 Pery Square,
Limerick; McCambridges, Mortons, Galway.

Moric Blaufränkisch
2012, Burgenland

TASTING NOTE
A superb, light, elegant wine, with piquant dark cherry and blueberry fruits.

DRINK WITH
Roast pork or chicken.

STYLE
Light and elegant

GRAPE VARIETY
Blaufränkisch

BACKSTORY
This is one of my all-time favourite wines, one that I beg people to try before dismissing Austrian red wines. Roland Velich is the man responsible for a revival of interest in Blaufränkisch in Austria. He makes a series of sophisticated, elegant wines with complex pure fruits and a mouth-watering mineral streak.

73 **Domaine Guillot Broux**
Bourgogne Pinot Noir 2012
France 12.5% **€23**

STOCKISTS: On the Grapevine, Dalkey; Cabot & Co, Westport;
Poppy Seed, Galway

Domaine Guillot Broux
Bourgogne Pinot Noir 2012

TASTING NOTE
Very pale in colour, fresh redcurrants and summer fruits with a lip-smackingly fresh quality.

DRINK WITH
Cold meats, salads and charcuterie

STYLE
Light and elegant

GRAPE VARIETY
Pinot Noir

BACKSTORY
Emmanuel Guillot Broux was born in the wrong place. Had he grown up an hour's drive further north, he would have inherited vineyards in the poshest, most expensive wine regions of Burgundy. His misfortune is our gain. Instead he fashions some of the most refined and elegant red and white wines in a region that produces masses of decent but unremarkable wine. As a result his prices are very reasonable given the quality.

74 Domaine des Roches Neuves
Saumur Champigny 2013
France 12.5% **€24.95**

STOCKISTS: Le Caveau, Kilkenny; Fallon & Byrne, Exchequer St.

Domaine des Roches Neuves
Saumur Champigny 2013

TASTING NOTE
Very moreish vivid redcurrant fruits with a smooth finish.
Perfect with all manner of cold meats.

DRINK WITH
Cold meats, patés and other charcuterie

STYLE
Light and elegant

GRAPE VARIETY
Cabernet Franc

BACKSTORY
Tired of big powerful red wines that leave your palate
exhausted after the first glass? If so, you could try a
Beaujolais, generally only around 13% in alcohol. Or a
Cabernet Franc from the Loire Valley; these wines are
light and refreshing with bright crunchy red fruits, lively
acidity and a tangy bite. On their own they can seem a little
austere, but with a plate of charcuterie, a few cheeses,
or any other medium-weight meat dishes, they are
wonderful. Serve cool for maximum enjoyment.

75

Carnuntum
2011 Muhr-van der Niepoort
Austria 13% **€24.99**

STOCKISTS: Greenacres, Wexford; Corkscrew, Chatham St; Redmonds, Ranelagh.

Carnuntum
2011 Muhr-van der Niepoort

TASTING NOTE
A fragrant nose and delicate, silky Pinotesque fruit -
red cherries and redcurrants - utterly delicious. 100%
Blaufränkisch.

DRINK WITH
Salmon, tuna, chicken and lighter pork dishes.

STYLE
Light and elegant

GRAPE VARIETY
Blaufränkisch

BACKSTORY
This is a true garagiste wine from a tiny winery operated
by Austria's P.R. guru Dorli Muhr in partnership with her
ex-husband Dirk Niepoort. He is better known as producer
of some of the greatest wines of the Douro Valley in
Portugal. The pair work together to create small quantities
of red wine in Carnuntum. The Austrian wines are subtle,
delicate and fragrant.

76

Dominio Bebei Lalama
Ribeira Sacra 2008
Spain 12.5% **€26.45**

STOCKISTS: Jus de Vine, Portmarnock; Donnybrook Fair;
The Wine Store: thewinestore.ie; 64wine, Glasthule.

Dominio Bebei Lalama
Ribeira Sacra 2008

TASTING NOTE
Superb, graceful, refined, mature, soft leafy dark fruits
that lap ever so gently around the mouth.

DRINK WITH
Roast game birds

STYLE
Light and elegant

GRAPE VARIETY
Mencia

BACKSTORY
This is one of the leading estates of Ribeira Sacra, an
ancient, very beautiful, but little known region that is
enjoying a revival. The Mencia grape has a wonderful
ability to taste good, young or old. Grown in various parts
of Galicia, and in Bierzo next door, it has a seductive,
savoury, sweet-sour quality and an alluring lightness.
Worth seeking it out.

77

Furst Spätburgunder
Tradition 2011, Baden
Germany 13% **€29.99**

STOCKISTS: On the Grapevine, Dalkey; Cabot & Co, Westport;
One Pery Sq, Limerick; 64wine, Glasthule..

Furst Spätburgunder
Tradition 2011, Baden

TASTING NOTE
Fragrant and soft with elegant, sweet dark cherry fruits.

DRINK WITH
Salmon, ham, or roast duck.

STYLE
Light and elegant

GRAPE VARIETY
Pinot Noir

BACKSTORY
German Pinot Noir, or Spätburgunder as it is known locally, has improved out of all recognition in the last decade. It is always light and delicate in style, but the best have a haunting bouquet and delicious soft silky fruits. Furst is generally reckoned to be one of the very best producers of Spätburgunder in Germany. I am in full agreement.

78

Alain Graillot
Crozes-Hermitage 2011
France 13% **€30**

STOCKISTS: 64wine, Glasthule; Jus de Vine, Portmarnock;
Mitchell & Son, IFSC & Sandycove.

Alain Graillot
Crozes-Hermitage 2011

TASTING NOTE
Violets on the nose with elegant, savoury, back cherry
fruits and layers of subtle liquorice and spice.

DRINK WITH
Roast game

STYLE
Light and elegant

GRAPE VARIETY
Syrah

BACKSTORY
Alain Graillot is one of the legendary winemakers of the
Northern Rhone. Lacking vineyards in the most sought-
after appellations, year after year he fashions some of
the most compelling wines of the entire Rhone Valley at
very reasonable prices. They can be drunk young but age
beautifully. Crozes-Hermitage has always been seen in
the shadow of Hermitage, one of the great wine names of
France. In recent years, a group of younger producers have
joined Graillot to make this an exciting region. Prices have
not quite caught up with quality yet.

79

Kasarí Areni Noir 2012,
Zorah
Armenia 14% **€34.99**

STOCKISTS: 64wine, Glasthule; Florries, Tramore; Mitchell's, IFSC and Glasthule; Red Nose, Clonmel; World Wide Wines, Waterford

Kasarí Areni Noir 2012,
Zorah

TASTING NOTE
Intriguing, lifted fragrant black cherries with good acidity and a light earthiness, finishing on a smooth note. Different and delicious wine.

DRINK WITH
Good with most medium-bodied white meat dishes.

STYLE
Light and elegant

GRAPE VARIETY
Areni Noir

BACKSTORY
Zorik Gharibian is an Iranian-Armenian who fled Iran following the revolution. Educated in the Armenian school on an island in Venice, he set up a successful fashion business in Milan where he lives with his wife and family. He began to visit Armenia following the collapse of the Soviet Union and became aware of an ancient lost wine culture. He set up his own vineyard using local grapes in a remote vineyard at 1,500 metres. "My ambition," he says, "is to make great wines of the highest international standard, to introduce Armenia's rich wine history and the potential of the treasure trove of Armenia's indigenous varieties to a diverse and worldwide audience. Time will tell if I succeed or not!"

80

Mas de Daumas Gassac 2011
IGP Haute Vallée du Gassac, Languedoc
France 13.5% €45

STOCKISTS: Red Nose Wine, Clonmel: rednosewine.com;
Curious Wines, Cork, Naas: curiouswines.ie; independent wine
shops.

Mas de Daumas Gassac 2011
IGP Haute Vallée du Gassac, Languedoc

TASTING NOTE
A wine that took on weight with every hour, offering
fine sophisticated red and dark fruits and an appealing
freshness, finishing with very fine-grained drying tannins.

DRINK WITH
Game, a plain roast of beef or lamb.

STYLE
Light and elegant

GRAPE VARIETY
80% Cabernet Sauvignon plus 20% "rare grape varieties",
according to the producer.

BACKSTORY
Mas de Daumas Gassac is a remarkable estate, created
back in the 1970s by Aimé Guibert. Today his family runs
this ambitious domaine, releasing a range of wines each
year. The white is also well worth trying. The estate is
located deep in the Languedoc with a unique combination
of soil and climate and the red wine has a character all of
its own. I tasted a flight (a number of different vintages)
of Daumas Gassac earlier this year going back several
decades; all were good and some sublime. One to enjoy
now or keep for a while.

ROUNDED AND FRUITY

81

Laurent Miquel
Syrah 2013, IGP pays d'Oc
France 13.5% **€9**

Laurent Miquel
Syrah 2013, IGP pays d'Oc

TASTING NOTE
Medium-bodied pure savoury plum fruits with a
touch of spice.

DRINK WITH
A good all-purpose wine to drink alongside most red and
white meat dishes.

STYLE
Rounded and fruity

GRAPE VARIETY
Syrah

BACKSTORY
As mentioned elsewhere in this book, Laurent Miquel
and his Irish wife, Neasa Corish, are responsible for an
amazing array of wines from the Languedoc. Standards
are high across the board, including the less expensive
wines. In fact, sometimes I prefer these as they haven't
been aged in oak barrels.

82

Protocolo 2012
VdT Castilla La Mancha
Spain 13.5% **€10.99**

STOCKISTS: O'Briens

Protocolo 2012
VdT Castilla La Mancha

TASTING NOTE
Soft, sweet, red cherry fruits crossed with vanilla
and spice.

DRINK WITH
Smooth and supple enough to serve at large parties,
but at its best with food - lighter red meats, such as
Irish Stew.

STYLE
Rounded and fruity

GRAPE VARIETY
Tempranillo

BACKSTORY
We all need them; a few fail-safe inexpensive red wines to
cheer up your stew on a wet Wednesday. If your penchant
is for Spanish reds this will deliver perfectly. I am not
promising a mind-blowing experience, but it won't damage
your wallet too much.

83

Domaine Bascou 2012
Cotes de Thongue
France 12.5% **€11.99**

STOCKISTS: O'Briens

Domaine Bascou 2012
Cotes de Thongue

TASTING NOTE
Supple forest fruits with a savoury kick and a smooth, easy finish.

DRINK WITH
Great with all kinds of medium-bodied red and white meat dishes.

STYLE
Rounded and fruity

GRAPE VARIETY
Syrah, Mourvedre

BACKSTORY
I have enjoyed the wines of Guy Bascou for more than two decades. Consistently well-made and easy to drink, they are always more than fairly priced. Perfect, reliable, everyday drinking.

84

Simone Joseph
Les Vignes Parallèles 2011
Côtes du Rhône
France 14.5% **€13.49**

STOCKISTS: 64wine, Glasthule; Jus de Vine, Portmarnock; Drink Store, Manor St; The Kitchen Project, Clonakilty; Cases, Galway.

Simone Joseph
Les Vignes Paralleles 2011
Côtes du Rhône

TASTING NOTE

A delicious wine that manages to combine a lovely fragrance and silky soft fruit with warming levels of alcohol.

DRINK WITH

Perfect with all red meats, roast, grilled or in a casserole.

STYLE

Rounded and fruity

GRAPE VARIETY

Grenache, Syrah, Cinsault

BACKSTORY

This is another of the Simone Joseph range produced by Simon Tyrrell, a winemaker and importer based in Ireland. His speciality is the Rhône Valley and it shows through in this wine. The Rhône is a huge appellation – basic Côtes du Rhône can run from flavourless through to seriously good wines at competitive prices, produced by a very talented new generation of winemakers. This is one of the latter.

85

El Castro de Valtuille 2013
Bierzo
Spain 14% **€13.50**

STOCKISTS: The Black Pig, Donnybrook; Baggot Street Wines; Red Island Wines, Skerries; Lilac Wines; Blackrock Cellar.

El Castro de Valtuille 2013
Bierzo

TASTING NOTE
Smooth, savory dark fruits and liquorice in a wine that slips down all too easily. Seriously good wine at an unbeatable price.

DRINK WITH
A good all-purpose wine to serve alongside medium-bodied meat, vegetables and cheese dishes.

STYLE
Rounded and fruity

GRAPE VARIETY
Mencía

BACKSTORY
Castro Ventosa is one of the largest producers in Bierzo in north-west Spain. They have been making wine since 1752. It helps that one family member is Raúl Pérez, recognised as one of the greatest winemakers in Spain today. This is their entry-level, unoaked wine. It is also one of my desert-island wines.

86 Leyda Pinot Noir 2011
Leyda Valley
Chile 14% **€13.99**

STOCKISTS: O'Briens

Leyda Pinot Noir 2011
Leyda Valley

TASTING NOTE
Bursting with soft, refreshing, ripe red cherry fruits and a smooth, rounded finish.

DRINK WITH
Grilled or roast chicken

STYLE
Rounded and fruity

GRAPE VARIETY
Pinot Noir

BACKSTORY
Viña Leyda was one of the pioneers in the Leyda Valley, source of many of the most exciting Chilean Pinot Noir and Sauvignon. I am a big Pinot Noir fan, constantly on the lookout for affordable bottles. This ranks amongst the very best value Pinots I have tasted over the last few years.

87

Secano Pinot Noir 2014
Leyda Valley
Chile 14.5% **€14.29**

STOCKISTS: Marks & Spencer

Secano Pinot Noir 2014
Leyda Valley

TASTING NOTE
A supple round wine with real power to match the sweet dark cherry fruits and spice..

DRINK WITH
Chicken or turkey.

STYLE
Rounded and fruity

GRAPE VARIETY
Pinot Noir

BACKSTORY
Made by the people who produce the Leyda Pinot Noir, featured on the previous pages. Marks & Spencer go to great lengths to source its wines, often employing its own winemakers. This is a special cuvee produced for them.

88

Santa Cristina
2013 IGT Toscana
Italy 13% **€14.99**

STOCKISTS: O'Briens; Dunnes Stores; Mortons of Galway;
Next Door Off-Licences.

Santa Cristina
2013 IGT Toscana

TASTING NOTE
Soft, rounded ripe cherry and blackcurrant fruits, with
very good length.

DRINK WITH
A good all-rounder to serve with white or red meats and
cheesy bakes.

STYLE
Rounded and fruity

GRAPE VARIETY
Sangiovese, Merlot

BACKSTORY
The Antinori family trace their roots back some 600 years,
but it is only the last few generations who have built the
company into one of the most formidable quality wine
producers in Italy. Like Torres in Spain, Antinori produces
a remarkable range of wines, including some of the most
sought-after in Italy. I have always enjoyed its basic Santa
Cristina, which no longer carries the Antinori name on the
label, a blend of the local Sangiovese with a little Merlot
to soften it out - a Chianti without the hard edges. It is the
sort of medium-bodied well-made wine you can imagine
drinking in a trattoria in Italy; a wine that improves both
mood and food, without ever setting the world alight.

89

Henri Nordoc
Cabernet Sauvignon
2012 Pays d'Oc
France 12.5% **€15**

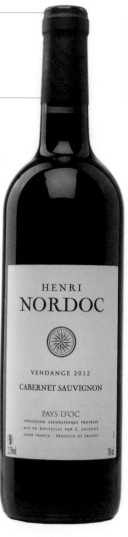

STOCKISTS: Le Caveau, Kilkenny; World Wide Wines, Waterford, The Corkscrew, Chatham St.

Henri Nordoc
Cabernet Sauvignon 2012 Pays d'Oc

TASTING NOTE
A very attractive warm climate Cab with tasty, juicy, ripe blackcurrant fruits and a lightly spicy finish. A bargain.

DRINK WITH
A good all-rounder to drink on a wet Wednesday with stews, pasta or grilled pork chops.

STYLE
Rounded and fruity

GRAPE VARIETY
Cabernet Sauvignon

BACKSTORY
I am not always a fan of Cabernet Sauvignon from the south of France; most of the time I prefer wines made from the more local Syrah, Grenache and Carignan. This wine, however, stood out in a line-up of inexpensive Cabernets from around the world.

90

Thymiopoulos
xinomavro 2013
Naoussa, Greece
Greece 14% **€13.79**

STOCKISTS: Marks & Spencer

Thymiopoulos
xinomavro 2013 Naoussa, Greece

TASTING NOTE
Delectably light and tangy but with rosehips and fresh,
piquant red fruits. Great with food.

DRINK WITH
Grilled or roast chicken

STYLE
Rounded and fruity

GRAPE VARIETY
Malagousia

BACKSTORY
Greek wine has fascinated me since I tasted an amazing
range of wines from various parts of the country ten years
ago. Forget all those preconceptions of retsina and cheap
holiday wine. These were great wines with a unique and
thrilling range of flavours. Since then I have made sure
to taste Greek wines at every opportunity. Over the last
18 months a few intrepid importers have started offering
these wines in Ireland. Both red and white can be delicious,
especially with food.

91

Les Grandes Vignes
Cotes du Rhone Villages 2012
France 14% **€15.45**

STOCKISTS: Jus de Vine, Portmarnock; The Drink Store,
Manor St; The Wine Store: thewinestore.ie

Les Grandes Vignes
Cotes du Rhone Villages 2012

TASTING NOTE
Bursting with refreshing juicy red cherry fruits, this is a delightful and dangerously moreish wine.

DRINK WITH
Grilled pork chops or chicken or great by itself.

STYLE
Rounded and fruity

GRAPE VARIETY
Cinsault

BACKSTORY
Not all wines from the Rhone are big muscular monsters. This tiny co-op produces some of the best-value wines in the entire Rhone Valley.

92

Degani
Valpolicella Classico DOC 2013
Italy 12.5% **€15.99**

STOCKISTS: Cabot & Co, Westport; On The Grapevine, Dalkey; Mortons of Galway; Listons, Camden St.

Degani
Valpolicella Classico DOC 2013

TASTING NOTE
Light, ripe, dark cherry fruits with a smooth, easy finish.

DRINK WITH
Light pasta dishes and pizza

STYLE
Rounded and fruity

GRAPE VARIETY
Corvina, Rondinella

BACKSTORY
What can we say about Valpolicella? Our parents drank
rivers of the cheap stuff at 1970s drinks parties and gave it a
very bad name. Modern Valpol is a different animal, brimful
with ripe juicy fruits and a tannin-free finish. This is light
enough to sip by itself, but would blend in effortlessly with
all kinds of salad dishes and cold meats as well as those
mentioned above.

93

Quinta Milú 2013
Ribera del Duero
Spain 13.5% **€16.70**

STOCKISTS: World Wide Wines, Waterford; 64wine, Glasthule; The Cheese Pantry, D7; Clontarf Wines; Listons, Camden Street; La Touche Wines, Greystones; Black Pig, Donnybrook; The Wine Workshop, Leeson St; Drinkstore, D7; Jus de Vine, Portmarnock.

Quinta Milú 2013
Ribera del Duero

TASTING NOTE
Pure piquant damson fruits, good acidity and a lightly tannic finish. Delicious.

DRINK WITH
Locally they would have this with roast lamb, a simple salad and good bread. Sounds great to me.

STYLE
Rounded and fruity

GRAPE VARIETY
Tempranillo

BACKSTORY
Ribera del Duero has become the Rolls Royce of Spanish wine over the last two decades. However, many producers equate quality with new oak, massive power and lots of alcohol. The Quinta Milú below is a welcome change; you hardly notice the oak (six months in French and Spanish barrels) amongst the enticing fresh dark fruits.

94

Domaine Elian Da Ros
Le Vin est une Fête, Côtes du
Marmandais 2012
France 12.5% **€16.95**

STOCKISTS: Terroirs, Donnybrook

Domaine Elian Da Ros
Le Vin est une Fête, Côtes du Marmandais 2012

TASTING NOTE
The name says it all - light, fresh and fruity, a wine that is
dangerously easy to drink.

DRINK WITH
Lighter meat dishes and salads. A great lunchtime wine.

STYLE
Rounded and fruity

GRAPE VARIETY
Abouriou, Cabernet Franc, Merlot

200

BACKSTORY
Having trained with leading Alsace producer Olivier
Humbrecht, Elian da Ros returned to take over the family
estate in the Marmandais. Working biodynamically, he has
quickly established himself as one of the brightest stars of
the region. Worth going out of your way to try.

95

Les Deux Cols 2013
Côtes du Rhône Cuvée d'Allizé
France 14.5% **€16.95**

STOCKISTS: 64wine, Glasthule; Jus de Vine, Portmarnock; Drink Store, Manor St; The Kitchen Project, Clonakilty; Cases, Galway.

Les Deux Cols 2013
Côtes du Rhône Cuvée d'Allizé

TASTING NOTE
Warm and full-bodied with clean, ripe strawberry and dark fruits.

DRINK WITH
Firm cheeses and pork dishes.

STYLE
Rounded and fruity

GRAPE VARIETY
Grenache, Syrah, Cinsault

BACKSTORY
This is a third Tyrrell production in the book, and certainly worthy of inclusion. The first 2012 vintage was very impressive and the 2013 is equally good. It would probably improve with a year's bottle age, but is very gluggable already.

96

Domaine de Sarabande
Misterioso 2012, Faugères
France 13.5% **€16.99**

Domaine de Sarabande
Misterioso 2012, Faugères

TASTING NOTE
Succulent and ripe, filled with dark cherry fruits dusted
with spices.

DRINK WITH
Grilled pork chops or other medium-bodied meat dishes.

STYLE
Rounded and fruity

GRAPE VARIETY
Grenache, Syrah

BACKSTORY
This estate was founded five years ago by Irishwoman Isla
Gordon and her Australian husband Paul Gordon. They
met in New Zealand where they worked for a number of
wineries. Isla concentrates on the viticulture, Paul on the
winemaking side of things. The domaine is in Faugeres, one
of the smaller appellations of the Languedoc. As well as
the Misterioso, made from a different blend each year, they
produce several other red wines and one of my favourite
rosés too.

97

Paço dos Cunhas de Santar 2010,
Dão (organic)
Portugal 14% **€15-17**

STOCKISTS: Sweeney's; Corkscrew; Baggot St Wines;
Clontarf Wines; Red Island Wines; McHugh.

Paço dos Cunhas de Santar 2010,
Dão (organic)

TASTING NOTE
Lovely wine with gentle, but concentrated, dark fruits and light fine-grained tannins on the finish.

DRINK WITH
Grilled pork chops or other medium-bodied meat dishes.

STYLE
Rounded and fruity

GRAPE VARIETY
Touriga Nacional, Alfrocheiro, Tinta Roriz

BACKSTORY
Dão has always intrigued me; apparently favoured by the dictator Salazar, it was always given special treatment and became the best-known region of Portugal. Sadly the wines didn't always hit the mark. However, these days there are plenty of ambitious producers making very good wine. The best have an intriguing delicacy and refreshing acidity that make them ideal with food.

98

Montepulciano d'Abruzzo
Zaccagnini dal Tracetto 2012
Italy 12.5% **€17.95**

STOCKISTS: Searsons, Monkstown; Jus de Vine,
Portmarnock; 1601 off-licence, Kinsale; Nolans, Clontarf;
The Wine Well, Dunboyne; Mortons, Ranelagh

Montepulciano d'Abruzzo
Zaccagnini dal Tracetto 2012

TASTING NOTE
Light, supple and full of dark cherry fruits with a twist on the finish.

DRINK WITH
Pizza, light pasta dishes

STYLE
Rounded and fruity

GRAPE VARIETY
Montepulciano

BACKSTORY
The wine with the twig wrapped around the bottle. Dreamt up 20 years ago, the vine cutting has become an instantly recognisable symbol. The wine is pretty good too!

99

La Stoppa
Trebbiolo 2012 IGT Emilia Rosso
Italy 13% **€19.60**

STOCKISTS: Le Caveau, Kilkenny; Fallon & Byrne, Exchequer St; Corkscrew, Chatham St; Ballymaloe Garden Shop; 64wine, Glasthule.

La Stoppa
Trebbiolo 2012 IGT Emilia Rosso

TASTING NOTE
Crunchy mouth-watering fresh damsons and
blackcurrants, with very light tannins. Serve cool.

DRINK WITH
Posh pizza or tomato-based pasta dishes.

STYLE
Rounded and fruity

GRAPE VARIETY
Barbera, Bonarda

BACKSTORY
The La Stoppa is one of the best natural wines I have come
across. I love the pure, clean freshness of the Barbera
grape; too often producers slather it with new oak.

100

Vigneti Zabù 'Il Passo'
Nerello Mascalese
2013, Sicily
Italy 13% **€19.99**

STOCKISTS: 64wine, Glasthule; Blackrock Cellar; Donnybrook Fair; The Drink Store, D7; Redmonds, Ranelagh; O'Briens; The Vineyard, Galway; Thomas, Foxrock; World Wide Wines, Waterford.

Vigneti Zabù 'Il Passo'
Nerello Mascalese 2013, Sicily

TASTING NOTE
Smooth, rich, dark fruits with roast coffee and spice.

DRINK WITH
This calls out for rich stews and roast red meats.

STYLE
Rounded and fruity

GRAPE VARIETY
Nerello Mascalese

BACKSTORY
Nerelo Mascalese is a uniquely Sicilian grape variety,
responsible for some of the great wines being produced
around Mount Etna. Usually the wines are elegant and
high in acidity; this wine has been given a lovely rich texture
through drying the grapes for a period before pressing.

101

Matetic Corralillo
Syrah 2011, San Antonio
Valley
Chile 14% **€19.99**

STOCKISTS: McCabes, Blackrock; Red Island Wines, Skerries;
Baggot Street Wines; Wines on the Green.

Matetic Corralillo
Syrah 2011, San Antonio Valley

TASTING NOTE
An exciting, very moreish, savoury wine with ripe damson fruits and a peppery kick on the finish.

DRINK WITH
Lamb, either grilled or stewed.

STYLE
Rounded and fruity

GRAPE VARIETY
Syrah

BACKSTORY
Matetic is one of the most extraordinary estates I have visited. The entire property is more than 15,000 hectares in size, with sheep and forestry the main business. The small winery produces some of Chile's very best wines, harmonious and sophisticated, with an appealing freshness. I once showed this wine to a group of Australian winemakers in the Barossa Valley; they couldn't believe Chile could produce Shiraz of this quality.

102 Dominio de Tares
Cepas Viejas 2009, Bierzo
Spain 14% **€24.50/£17.50**

STOCKISTS: James Nicholson, Crossgar: jnwine.com

Dominio de Tares
Cepas Viejas 2009, Bierzo

TASTING NOTE
Seductive, rounded, ripe dark cherries with a subtle
spiciness and a pleasing meaty character.

DRINK WITH
Grilled red meats or firm cheeses.

STYLE
Rounded and fruity

GRAPE VARIETY
Mencía

BACKSTORY
I have listed a few wines made from the Mencia grape.
Grown in the north-western corner of Spain, it makes
intriguing wines with an attractive sweet-sour character.
This has more meaty substance than the others, but is
equally enjoyable.

103

COS Cerasuolo di Vitorria
2010, Sicily
Italy 13% **€29.99**

STOCKISTS: On the Grapevine, Dalkey; Cabot & Co, Westport; 64wine, Glasthule; No 1 Pery Square, Limerick; Jus de Vine, Portmarnock; The Corkscrew, Chatham Street.

COS Cerasuolo di Vitorria
2010, Sicily

TASTING NOTE
A wonderful floral nose with juicy ripe dark cherry and raspberry fruits, good depth and an attractive subtle earthy touch.

DRINK WITH
Most white and lighter red meat dishes

STYLE
Rounded and fruity

GRAPE VARIETY
Frappato, Nero d'Avola

BACKSTORY
Originally there were three partners in COS; each had an initial that together made up the name. In a beautifully designed modern winery in Sicily they were the youngest winemakers in Italy back in 1980. Giusto Ochipinti and Giambattista (Titta) Cilia (the 'o' and the 'c' in COS) have since redefined everything about the area, using biodynamic practices, ancient clay amphorae and traditional grape varieties. A friend once described their wonderful Cerasuolo di Vittoria as 'a soft velvet cushion'. It isn't cheap but I find it a hugely harmonious and satisfying wine.

104

Felton Road
Pinot Noir 2012,
Central Otago
New Zealand 14% **€49**

FELTON ROAD

FELTON ROAD
ESTABLISHED 1991

Bannockburn
PINOT NOIR
CENTRAL OTAGO
2012

PRODUCED AND BOTTLED BY
FELTON ROAD WINES LTD
BANNOCKBURN

GRAPES GROWN AT OUR BANNOCKBURN VINEYARDS

Wine of New Zealand

STOCKISTS: On The Grapevine, Dalkey; Cabot and Co,
Westport; The Corkscrew, Chatham Street.

Felton Road
Pinot Noir 2012, Central Otago

TASTING NOTE
Elegant, yet intensely flavoured, with lifted pure dark cherry fruits and a cleansing acidity. Very different to Burgundy but an excellent wine.

DRINK WITH
Roast duck, wild or farmed.

STYLE
Rounded and fruity

GRAPE VARIETY
Pinot Noir

BACKSTORY
Central Otago has the most southerly vineyards in the world. Twenty years ago there was nothing here but sheep. Now it is the most talked-about region in New Zealand for Pinot Noir. An English Burgundy fanatic, Nigel Greening, bought Felton Road with a view to producing top quality Pinot Noir. He has succeeded.

RICH AND FULL-BODIED

105

La Tribu 2012
Valencia
Spain 14% **€13**

223

STOCKISTS: Clontarf Wines; 64wine; Michaels, Deerpark;
Listons; Wicklow Wine Co; Drinkstore.

La Tribu 2012
Valencia

TASTING NOTE
A beautifully soft, ripe, plump wine with sultry dark fruits.

DRINK WITH
A glugger to enjoy with a barbeque or more roubust fare in the winter months.

STYLE
Rich and full-bodied

GRAPE VARIETY
Monastrell, Syrah

BACKSTORY
Valencia always had a reputation for volume and big, clumsy, powerful red wines that could be sold as Spanish table wine, or even (illegally) used to beef up Rioja. Rafael Cambra is a thoughtful winemaker; based high up in the mountains, behind the resorts of Valencia. In these cooler vineyards (although still very hot at times), he manages to produce wines with voluptuous, smooth, ripe dark fruits, often at ridiculously cheap prices.

106

Atlantico Sur
Tannat 2011
Uruguay 13.5% **€15.49**

STOCKISTS: O'Briens

Atlantico Sur
Tannat 2011

TASTING NOTE
Good, deeply satisfying wine with firm, dark ripe fruits
and a dry finish.

DRINK WITH
Beef in all its forms. Barbecued steak would be perfect.

STYLE
Rich and full-bodied

GRAPE VARIETY
Tannat

BACKSTORY
Tannat is tannic, or so we are always told. Originally from
the south-west corner of France, where it makes deep,
impenetrable, dark wines, it was brought by French
immigrants to Uruguay, where it is the most popular grape.
Here it retains some of its tannic bite, but with very crowd-
pleasing ripe fruits too.

107

Doña Paula Estate
Uco Valley Malbec 2012
Argentina 14.2% **€15.99**

STOCKISTS: Widely available, including O'Briens, SuperValu and Tesco.

Doña Paula Estate
Uco Valley Malbec 2012

TASTING NOTE

Intense aromas of violets followed by rich cassis, loganberries and vanilla spice on the palate. An intriguing combination of power and elegance.

DRINK WITH

A nice steak, but it is more versatile than that - very good with most red and white meats or firm cheese.

STYLE

Rich and full-bodied

GRAPE VARIETY

Malbec

BACKSTORY

Malbec is a French grape, but it was brought to Argentina over a century ago. Here it has thrived, producing wines rich in fruit but with a trademark juiciness that makes it dangerously easy to drink.

108 Domaine de Fondrèche
'Fayard' 2012, Ventoux
France 14% **€18.65**

STOCKISTS: Donnybrook Fair; The Wine Store: thewinestore.ie

Domaine de Fondrèche
'Fayard' 2012, Ventoux

TASTING NOTE
A wonderfully smooth, rich, ripe red with real finesse.

DRINK WITH
Red meats, grilled pork.

STYLE
Rich and full-bodied

GRAPE VARIETY
Grenache, Syrah, Mourvedre

BACKSTORY
Sebastien Vincenti produces a series of knockout wines, made using organic and biodynamic methods. The unique microclimate, on a plateau in the Ventoux, seems to be partly responsible for the amazing mix of freshness and minerality on the one hand, and rich, velvety power on the other.

109

Willunga 100
McLaren Vale
Grenache 2013
Australia 14.5% **€18.49**

STOCKISTS: Blackrock Cellar; Bradleys, Cork; Cases, Galway;
Jus de Vine, Portmarnock; Florries, Tramore; La Touche,
Greystones; Martins, Fairview; No.21, Kinsale; O'Briens;
Wicklow Wine Co; wineonline.ie; World Wide Wines, Waterford.

Willunga 100
McLaren Vale Grenache 2013

TASTING NOTE
Full-bodied and soft with delicious strawberries and
spice. The perfect winter warmer.

DRINK WITH
Rich stews and casseroles.

STYLE
Rich and full-bodied

GRAPE VARIETY
Grenache

BACKSTORY
Grenache (or Garnacha in its native Spain) produces a
variety of styles, but as the grapes don't really properly ripen
until it hits a potential of at least 14%, they always have
heart-warming levels of alcohol. Classic Grenache has soft,
rounded, strawberry fruits and very low levels of tannin -
dangerously easy to drink during cold weather or with a
barbecue.

110

Meandro do Vale Meao
2011, Douro
Portugal 14.5% **€20.95**

STOCKISTS: La Touche Wines, Greystones; Donnybrook
Fair; Corkscrew; Fallon & Byrne; Fresh; Mortons; Listons;
Deveney's; Coachouse; Sweeney's; McGuinness, Dundalk;
Nectar.

Meandro do Vale Meao
2011, Douro

TASTING NOTE
A fragrant nose with elegant, slightly earthy dark fruits
that open out nicely with time.

DRINK WITH
Rich stews and casseroles.

STYLE
Rich and full-bodied

GRAPE VARIETY
Touriga Nacional, Touriga Franca, Tinta Roriz

BACKSTORY
Quinta do Vale Meao is one of the legendary wines of
Portugal. The grapes from this estate were once used to
make Barca Velha, an even more legendary wine, but this
brand-name is now owned by another wine producer. Still
with me? Now all of the best grapes, from single vineyards
along the stunning Douro Valley, go into the Quinta wine
which sells for around €80. Those not considered quite
good enough are used to make this wine. That way we get to
taste a junior version of a great wine at half the price. Worth
trying.

111

Ch. Milhau-Lacugue
Saint Chinian
"Les Truffieres" 2010
France 14.5% **€20.95**

235

STOCKISTS: The Corkscrew, Chatham St; The Coach House, Balinteer; Probus Wines, Fenian Street, D2; Searsons, Monkstown; Terroirs, Donnybrook; The Wicklow Wine Co.

Ch. Milhau-Lacugue
Saint Chinian "Les Truffieres" 2010

TASTING NOTE
Rich and deeply-flavoured with dense dark fruits,
herbs of the garrigue; boldly uncompromising and very
satisfying.

DRINK WITH
Red meats, game.

STYLE
Rich and full-bodied

GRAPE VARIETY
Syrah, Grenache

BACKSTORY
This wine was completely unknown to me when I first tasted
it early this year. It blew me away with its complex flavours
and huge personality. I subsequently found out that it was
a highly rated wine in Saint Chinian, itself a part of the
Langeudoc that is responsible for some great wines. So no
surprise really, but a great discovery.

112 Mendel Malbec 2011
Mendoza
Argentina 14.5% **€22.99**

STOCKISTS: Wines on the Green; Jus de Vine, Portmarnock;
The Black Pig, Donnybrook; Blackrock Cellars.

Mendel Malbec 2011
Mendoza

TASTING NOTE
Restrained dark fruit aromas, plush ripe sweet fruits, and a beautifully integrated long finish.

DRINK WITH
The books would say steak and they have a point. But a roast of beef or lamb would be equally good.

STYLE
Rich and full-bodied

GRAPE VARIETY
Malbec

BACKSTORY
Mendel is not the best-known name in Mendoza; however I have taken part in several blind tastings where it has done consistently well. As with all of the best wines from this part of the world, there is a perfect balance of power and freshness. The rich, oaky, white Semillon is also delicious and the various red wines are all worth trying.

113

Achaval Ferrer
Malbec 2011, Mendoza
Argentina 14.5%
€24.69/£17.95

239

ACHAVAL FERRER

Malbec
2011

MENDOZA

ARGENTINA

STOCKISTS: James Nicholson, Crossgar: jnwine.com

Achaval Ferrer
Malbec 2011, Mendoza

TASTING NOTE
Very enticing pure fruits on the nose, followed by a
beautifully elegant, lightly spicy palate with clean fresh
loganberries, smooth tannins and a very good finish.

DRINK WITH
Barbecued steak would be traditional but any roast or
grilled red meat would do very nicely.

STYLE
Rich and full-bodied

GRAPE VARIETY
Malbec

BACKSTORY
Achaval Ferrer produces some of Argentina's finest wines,
including three highly sought-after single vineyard wines.
It was founded in 1998 by a small group of Argentine wine
lovers and renowned Italian winemaker Roberto Cipresso.

114

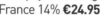

Domaine d'Aupilhac 2011
Montpeyroux, Languedoc
France 14% **€24.95**

STOCKISTS: Blackrock Cellar; Coach House, Ballinteer;
The Corkscrew, Chatham St; On the Grapevine, Dalkey;
Hollands, Bray; Probus Wines, Fenian St; 64wine, Glasthule;
Pettitt's, Wexford; The Wicklow Wine Co.

Domaine d'Aupilhac 2011
Montpeyroux, Languedoc

TASTING NOTE
Firm, concentrated, earthy dark fruits in a cloak of drying tannins. Decant and enjoy or keep a few years.

DRINK WITH
Grilled red meats

STYLE
Rich and full-bodied

GRAPE VARIETY
Mourvedre, Syrah, Carignan, Grenache, Cinsault

BACKSTORY
One of the great winemakers of the Languedoc, Sylvan Fadat pursued the path of quality long before others dared in a region renowned for inexpensive glugging wines. He is deeply imbedded in the locality and his wines exude character and personality. The best reds are full of complex fruits, herbs and firm tannins, wines to lay down, or decant an hour before dinner. But certainly worth trying.

115

Colomé
Malbec 2012, Cafayate
Argentina 14.5% **€24.99**

STOCKISTS: Blackrock Cellar; Clontarf Wines; Deveney's, Dundrum; Donnybrook fair; Fallon & Byrne, Exchequer St; Redmond's, Ranelagh; Jus de Vine, Portmarnock; Mitchell & Son, IFSC & Sandycove; The Corkscrew, Chatham St; Thomas Woodberry, Galway.

Colomé
Malbec 2012, Cafayate

TASTING NOTE
A brilliant wine, ripe yet muscular, packed full with
loganberry and plum fruits.

DRINK WITH
The standard choice would be a steak, but any grilled red
meat or roast game would work very well.

STYLE
Rich and full-bodied

GRAPE VARIETY
Malbec

BACKSTORY
This claims to be the highest vineyard in the world. I didn't
make it to the summit, but the wine does. An amazing
combination of rippling fruit, minerals and power.

116

Rosso di Montalcino 2012
Canalicchio di Sopra
Italy 14% **€26.50**

STOCKISTS: Sheridans (Dublin, Galway, Carnaross, Co.Meath): sheridanscheesemongers.com; The Wine Workshop, Dublin.

Rosso di Montalcino 2012
Canalicchio di Sopra

TASTING NOTE
Seriously good Rosso di Montalcino with concentrated, cool, dark cherry fruits, an earthy edge and firm, dry tannins on the finish.

DRINK WITH
Grilled or roast red meats

STYLE
Rich and full-bodied

GRAPE VARIETY
Sangiovese

BACKSTORY
There are times when I give up on Montalcino; there are so many versions and not all are good. The American market demands big, extracted, over-ripe, over-oaked wines. Others are too tannic and dry. Just occasionally you come across a really good one and understand what the fuss is all about. This wine, a lowly Rosso di Montalcino as opposed to Vino Nobile, is one such example.

117

Taltarni Shiraz 2008
Heathcote, Victoria
Australia 14.5% **€26.99**

247

STOCKISTS: O'Briens

Taltarni Shiraz 2008
Heathcote, Victoria

TASTING NOTE
A beguiling combination of power and ripeness on one hand with a cool elegance on the other. Maturing nicely.

DRINK WITH
Roast beef or lamb or maybe a big juicy hamburger.

STYLE
Rich and full-bodied

GRAPE VARIETY
Shiraz

BACKSTORY
The vines are planted on 500 million-year-old crushed volcanic rock giving an amazing depth and intensity of flavour. Once a busy mining town, Heathcote is now renowned for Shiraz that combines great concentration and power with silky smooth tannins. It is a rare treat to find an Australian wine of this maturity.

FORTIFIED

118

Delgado Zuleta
"La Goya" Manzanilla Sherry
Spain 15% **€11** [half-bottle]

STOCKISTS: Black Pig, Donnybrook; 64wine, Glasthule;
Red Island, Skerries; Clontarf Wines; The Wicklow Wine Co;
Blackrock Cellar; Baggot Street Wines; Jus de Vine; Listons;
Sweeneys, Ennis [SCR]

Delgado Zuleta
"La Goya" Manzanilla Sherry

TASTING NOTE
Deliciously tangy, saline, dry wine brimming with racy citrus and almonds

DRINK WITH
Tapas; Iberico ham works really well as does crab salad.

STYLE
Fortified

GRAPE VARIETY
Palamino Fino

BACKSTORY
This is the flagship wine of Delgado Zuleta, one of the oldest sherry firms still in existence. Manzanilla, made in the seaside town of Sanlucar de Barrameda, is even lighter and fresher than a standard Fino sherry. This is one of the very best, and comes in a very handy 1/2 bottle - perfect for two before dinner - or one thirsty wine writer. Always serve chilled.

119

Hidalgo Pastrana
Manzanilla Pasada Sherry
Spain 15% **€22.25/£15.99**

STOCKISTS: James Nicholson, Crossgar: jnwine.com

Hidalgo Pastrana
Manzanilla Pasada Sherry

TASTING NOTE
One of the greatest sherries of all. Intense nuts, olives and umami.

DRINK WITH
A fino or manzanilla should be drunk chilled with oily fish, serrano ham, olives, toasted almonds, tortilla and any other spanish delicacy.

STYLE
Fortified

GRAPE VARIETY
Palamino Fino

BACKSTORY
Unique in several ways. Made with grapes from the Pastrana vineyard that has been owned by the Hidalgo family for several hundred years, this is aged in cask for an extended period. Possibly not suited to those starting to taste sherry, but one of the most delicious and complex of all.

120

Equipo Navajos La Fino
Macharnudo Alto Bota
54 Sherry
Spain 15% **€30.99**

STOCKISTS: Wines on the Green, Dawson St; Black Pig, Donnybrook; Blackrock Cellar; Jus de Vin, Portmarnock; Drinkstore, D7; Baggot Street Wines; 64wine, Glasthule.

Equipo Navajos La Fino
Macharnudo Alto Bota 54 Sherry

TASTING NOTE
Packed with intensely complex flavours of nuts, lemon and yeast and finishes deliciously crisp, dry and refreshing.

DRINK WITH
Serve chilled with Iberico ham and other light tapas.

STYLE
Fortified

GRAPE VARIETY
Palamini Fino

BACKSTORY
This is the first of two wines from the Equipo Navajas team (see No 122). I tasted this, served well-chilled, in the hot summer sun of Jerez. It is an incredible wine that simply explodes with flavour.

121 Barbeito
10 year-old Sercial
Reserve Madeira
Portugal 19% **€35**

STOCKISTS: Wines on the Green; Jus de Vin, Portmarknock;
McCabes, Blackrock; 64wine, Glasthule; Redmonds,
Ranelagh; Clontarf Wines.

Barbeito
10 year-old Sercial Reserve Madeira

TASTING NOTE
Dryish, tangy dried fruit and orange zest with a hint of grilled nuts.

DRINK WITH
I like to serve the Sercial, the driest Madeira, lightly chilled before dinner or with patés and soups.

STYLE
Fortified

GRAPE VARIETY
Sercial

BACKSTORY
Madeira is probably the least known of the three major fortified wines. It can be quite difficult to find, and the quality is not always what it should be; a pity as this can be one of the world's great wines. There is a fantastic and unique tangy orange-peel intensity to all the best examples. As it goes through a special "cooking" process, Madeira is nigh-on indestructible. An opened bottle will keep for months - provided it lasts that long of course.

122

Equipo Navajos
La Bota 37 Amontillado
Sherry
Spain 18.5% **€53.99**

EQUIPO NAVAZOS

LA BOTA DE
AMONTILLADO

37 "Navazos"

Sanlúcar

STOCKISTS: Wines on the Green; Jus de Vine, Portmarnock;
The Black Pig, Donnybrook; Blackrock Cellars.

Equipo Navajos
La Bota 37 Amontillado Sherry

TASTING NOTE
A stunning sherry with an amazing intensity of salty caramel, orange peel and grilled nuts. The finish lasts minutes.

DRINK WITH
Amontillado is the perfect accompaniment to cold meat, pies and pâtés. Locally it is frequently drunk with kidneys cooked in amontillado. Serve chilled.

STYLE
Fortified

GRAPE VARIETY
Palamino

BACKSTORY
This is the second of two wines (see No 120) from Equipo Navajas which has been the talk of the sherry world in recent years. Criminology lecturer Jésus Barquin and Eduardo Ojeda founded the company in 2005. They taste many old barrels of wine and buy specific cuvées from different producers. They are amongst the best sherries you can buy. Each release is from a single barrel and is given a unique number.

123

Taylors
20-Year-Old Tawny Port
Portugal 20% **€59.95**

STOCKISTS: Bradleys, Cork; The Castle Off-licence; Deveny's, Rathmines & Dundrum; McHugh's, Kilbarrack & Artane; Sweeney's, Glasnevin; The Corkscrew, Chatham St; La Touche, Greystones; O'Briens; Select SuperValu.

Taylors
20-Year-Old Tawny Port

TASTING NOTE
Light cherry fruits overlaid with caramel, dried fruits and
toasted nuts, finishing very nicely on a long off-dry note.

DRINK WITH
Lightly chilled with patés and terrines, firm cheeses, or
with fruit tarts.

STYLE
Fortified

GRAPE VARIETY
Touriga Nacional, Touriga Francesa, Tinta Barroca

BACKSTORY
Tawny ports have been aged in cask for years. Unlike vintage
port they require no decanting. Served lightly chilled, they
make a great accompaniment to all kinds of food, sweet and
savoury.